Cambridge Computer Science Texts · 4

Macro Processors

A. J. COLE

Department of Computational Science
University of St Andrews, Fife, Scotland

Cambridge University Press
CAMBRIDGE
LONDON · NEW YORK · MELBOURNE

Published by the Syndics of the Cambridge University Press

The Pitt Building, Trumpington Street, Cambridge CB2 1RP

Bentley House, 200 Euston Road, London NW1 2DB

32 East 57th Street, New York, NY 10022, USA

296 Beaconsfield Parade, Middle Park, Melbourne 3206, Australia

First published 1976

Printed in Great Britain

at the University Printing House, Cambridge

(Euan Phillips, University Printer)

Library of Congress Cataloging in Publication Data

Cole, Alfred John.
    Macro processors.

    (Cambridge computer science texts ; 5)
    Includes bibliographies and index.
    1. Macro processors. I. Title. II. Series.
QA76.6.C625   001.6'42   75-19576

ISBN 0 521 29024 4

Contents

		page
Preface		v
Chapter 1	INTRODUCTION	
1.1	Informal development	1
1.2	Definitions	7
1.3	Some general concepts	12
1.4	Summary	18
1.5	Bibliography	19
Chapter 2	ASSEMBLER LANGUAGE MACRO PROCESSING	
2.1	Introduction	20
2.2	A choice of assembler language	21
2.3	Macro definition	26
2.4	Simple parameters	27
2.5	Keyword parameters	30
2.6	Parameter lists	32
2.7	Conditional assembly	33
2.8	Conditional assembly data types	39
2.9	Attributes	41
2.10	System macros	45
2.11	Summary	45
2.12	Bibliography	46
2.13	Examples	47
Chapter 3	STRING HANDLING MACRO PROCESSORS	
3.1	Introduction	49
3.2	A general description of TRAC	50
3.3	A formal description of the TRAC algorithm	59

3.4	Some hints on implementing the TRAC algorithm	61
3.5	Some TRAC examples	62
3.6	The remaining TRAC functions	63
3.7	Some further TRAC examples	69
3.8	A brief description of GPM	74
3.9	The internal structure of GPM	81
3.10	An introduction to ML/I	85
3.11	The LOWL language and its use in implementing software	99
3.12	Conclusion	105
3.13	Bibliography	107
3.14	Examples	108

Chapter 4	A MOBILE PROGRAMMING SYSTEM	
4.1	Introduction	110
4.2	The SIMCMP algorithm	113
4.3	The FLUB machine	119
4.4	The STAGE2 macro processor	125
4.5	Conclusion	130
4.6	Bibliography	131
4.7	Examples	131

Chapter 5	MP/3 - A TOP END MACRO PROCESSOR WITH SYSTEM FACILITIES	
5.1	Introduction	133
5.2	The basic notation and features of MP/3	134
5.3	The matching and expansion of macro calls	144
5.4	Chains and structures of chains	150
5.5	Integration of MP/3 with other systems	155
5.6	Some applications of MP/3	156
5.7	Conclusion	157
5.8	Bibliography	158
5.9	Examples	158

Chapter 6   A BOOT STRAPPED LIST PROCESSING SYSTEM

6.1   Introduction   160

6.2   WISP   161

6.3   A simple compiler for WISP   166

6.4   Code generation for a Fortran version of   171
the WISP compiler

6.5   Conclusion   176

6.6   Bibliography   176

6.7   Examples   177

Chapter 7   SYNTAX MACROS

7.1   Introduction   178

7.2   Basic concepts and definitions   184

7.3   Syntax macros at the syntactic analysis   186
phase

7.4   Code macros   189

7.5   Summary   197

7.6   Bibliography   199

7.7   Examples   199

Chapter 8   SOME APPLICATIONS OF SYNTAX MACROS TO
EXTENSIBLE COMPILERS

8.1   Introduction   201

8.2   BALM - an extendible list processing   202
language

8.3   A user extensible language built on to a   210
compiler compiler

8.4   An extension mechanism for LL(1) languages   214

8.5   Conclusions   221

8.6   Bibliography   222

Index   224

Preface

The Cambridge Computer Science Texts are intended for use
in undergraduate courses in Computer Science both in Univer-
sities and Colleges of Technology. The subject matter in this
book has formed the basis of a course on macro processors
which has been given annually in the University of St. Andrews
over the past six years. Naturally the course has developed
in both breadth and depth during these years but the subject
matter covered here can be quite easily covered in about
twenty lectures at the Honours level provided that the stu-
dents are expected to read additional material from time to
time.

Many macro processors have been written in the past ten
or fifteen years and some ten of these are described in this
book. It is not intended that this text should consist of a
shopping list of available macro processors, nor is it intended to be a collection of users' manuals. The intention has
been to discuss the purpose of the various systems and in particular to describe their internal structure rather than to
give detailed and intimate instructions as to their use. Such
detail together with pathological examples of their more esoteric capabilities can usually be found in their authors' guide
to system use for more advanced programmers, which has frequently been the basis of a doctoral thesis aimed more perhaps
at impressing the examiners rather than the user. In most
cases the reader who wishes seriously to use one of the macro
processors described in this book, or indeed in any of the many
whose description is not included here, would do better to read

and understand first the Simple (which usually has an implied meaning of 'idiot's') Guide rather than go immediately to the full blooded, bells and whistles version. The principle involved here is that it is better to understand fully the basic premises rather than to misunderstand the general theory.

The internal structure of a macro processor is interesting even if the reader has no serious intention of using the processor itself to solve practical problems since many of the ideas used are of value in other contexts. For example, the basically simple but nevertheless powerful scanning algorithms used in some of the string manipulation processors are models of economic yet versatile programming.

A reasonable knowledge of high level programming languages is all that is really required for the understanding of the first six chapters. Chapters 7 and 8 require some knowledge of the basic principles of compiling techniques with particular reference to syntax analysers, but even here such required knowledge is fairly primitive and if the course on macro processors is given at the end of the first or beginning of the second year of an honours course then most computer science departments will have covered far more than is required here.

Although most of this book formed the basis of lecture notes much of the actual text was prepared during sabbatical leave at the University of Grenoble and I am indebted to Professors Bolliet and Griffiths for the use of their facilities and to M. Max Peltier who at the time was Director of the IBM Scientific Centre at Grenoble and to his staff for many interesting and fruitful discussions.

I am also indebted to my research student Mr. Bill Campbell who has debugged the text and made many helpful suggestions including in particular examples on the use of the language extension capabilities in the language BALM.

My sympathy and thanks are also extended to my secretary

Mrs. Maureen Sanders who has had to cope with my writing which gets smaller and more illegible as midnight approaches and passes.

Finally a word of advice to the reader. Although this book could be read without writing a single macro or consulting a single reference the gain would be proportional to the effort. As a first reference you should immediately read and act on James, 1,22.

A.J.C.

1 · Introduction

1.1 *Informal development*

A common problem which occurs in the writing of computer programs is the tedious one of repetition of whole pieces of text in different parts of the same program. If these are sufficiently large and general then the usual solution is to write a procedure or subroutine in which the formal parameters used at declaration time are replaced by actual parameters at run time. This solution is quite satisfactory if the code body of the procedure is sufficiently large to warrant the time and space used in setting up the procedure linkage and parameter passing mechanisms. Since compilers are usually designed to be as general as possible it often happens that quite complicated linkage mechanisms are established for every procedure and the consequent overhead is very high even for the simplest of procedures. As a matter of interest the reader should try compiling either an Algol procedure with appropriate procedure heading and code body

    begin
    end

or a Fortran subroutine with body

    END

to see just what the system overhead is in his own laboratory.

Suppose for example we are programming in Algol the solution to a problem which involves the repeated use of stacks. Quite frequently we will wish to put an item on the stack and increment the stack pointer. Thus on one occasion we may have to write

```
STACK(PTR) := ITEM;
PTR := PTR + 1;
```

and on another occasion

```
STACK1 (PNTR) := X;
PNTR := PNTR + 1;
```

We could of course write a procedure to handle this but as we have already indicated this can be quite inefficient. What we really need is a simple method of planting *in-line code* in the program so that a statement such as

```
PUSH (STACK, PTR, ITEM);
```

produces the in-line code

```
STACK(PTR) := ITEM;

PTR := PTR + 1;
```

as if the programmer had actually written this himself.

A similar problem in a different context arises in assembler language programming in which very frequently a large number of declarative statements have to be written at the beginning of an assembler language program, one for each variable to be used in the subsequent program. It could well be argued that this is a deficiency in the programming language but even though such criticism may be a relief to the pent up feelings of the programmer it does not relieve the tedium of writing, punching and subsequently correcting errors in two hundred statements of the form

    DS X

where the symbols have to be punched in the correct field of a card if they are not to be rejected by the assembler. It would be very attractive if one could simply write

    DEFSYM(X,Y,Z,THIS,THAT,MINE,PQ1T,SPIT,ETC)

and have a list of the corresponding declarative statements produced automatically.

Problems such as these gave rise to the idea of macro processors. As with all good ideas in programming the effect of the introduction of a solution to a simple problem of this nature has been much wider than was originally visualised and the purpose of this book is to describe some of these ideas and in particular the way in which they have been implemented.

In the next section of this chapter we will formally define some of the terms which have become associated with the theory of macro processors but first of all we will informally discuss some of these and also give an example of the use of macros in a different area, namely that of text replacement.

Before using a macro we must firstly define it in a similar manner to the definition of a procedure and the associated procedure body. A typical macro definition of the first example given above could be

    $MACRODEF
    PUSH($1,$2,$3).

```
    $1($2) :=$3;
    $2:=$2+1;
    $MACROEND
```

Here the words MACRODEF and MACROEND delimit the definition,
and the line of code

```
    PUSH($1,$2,$3).
```

defines the form of a subsequent call of this macro.

This line of code is called a *macro template* and the
symbols $1, $2, $3 are the formal parameters. The full stop
indicates the end of the template definition but is not normally used in a subsequent macro call which typically would be

```
    PUSH(STACK, PTR, ITEM)
```

The next two lines of code, namely,

```
    $1($2):=$3;
    $2 :=$2+1;
```

make up the macro body and generate the in-line code

```
    STACK(PTR) := ITEM;
    PTR := PTR + 1;
```

to *replace* the macro call

```
    PUSH(STACK, PTR, ITEM)
```

in the main body of the program.

The idea of the use of a macro processor as an adjoint
to computer languages is not new. Greenwald (1959) and McIlroy

(1960), amongst others, published papers on the subject but the basic ideas were already in use before that time by various computer manufacturers to assist in the production of systems programs and were usually used in conjunction with an assembly language.

Over the years descriptions of a large number of pieces of software loosely described as macro processors have been published. Because of the diversity of implementations and use of these pieces of software it is difficult to give a formal definition of a macro processor which will cover all of them. However, one common feature is that of text replacement and although not all programs which replace certain textual patterns by other previously defined or automatically generated pieces of text can be described as macro processors, the inverse is certainly true. We will therefore consider text replacement to be the distinguishing property of macro processors.

Brown (1969) defines for his purposes a macro processor as "a piece of software designed to allow the user to add new facilities of his own design to an existing piece of software". This definition gives the flavour of macro processing but is as unsatisfactory as ours in the sense that it is too wide.

It is almost certainly not worthwhile to try to develop a watertight definition of a macro processor. Like so many other concepts in mathematics or computer science it is one which clarifies itself as use is made of it and a formal definition is more likely to confuse the beginner rather than to help him. One can not of course draw the conclusion that formal definition is never necessary since frequently it is essential to delimit the application area of a concept. In our case this is not necessary and we are not worried if marginal cases are included or excluded.

We referred above to text replacement and the idea here can vary from a very simple substitution of fixed replacement text for fixed sequences of characters to complex generation of replacement text using parameters of various types and possibly internal definition and nested calls of other macros or indeed of itself.

As a simple example consider some future edition of the University of St.Andrews Calendar in which all references to the "Chair of Applied Mathematics" are to be replaced by "Chairs of Applied Mathematics and Frisbology". We note immediately an ambiguity in the language we have used. The intention is to replace the four words Chair of Applied Mathematics by the corresponding six words Chairs of Applied Mathematics and Frisbology. The quotation marks were only used as a notation to delimit the phrases in the description above and are not expected to appear in the Calendar. Furthermore the words "of Applied Mathematics" are not replaced but are *displaced* one character to the right to accommodate an additional "s" on the word "Chair". Despite the fact that the words "of Applied Mathematics" have not really been replaced we still refer to this type of substitution as text replacement.

Note also that we have to look for the whole phrase "Chair of Applied Mathematics" and not just for the words "Applied Mathematics" even though the Chair was not to be duplicated; that is, even though there was only to be a single Chair with the title "Chair of Applied Mathematics and Frisbology". If we were only to look for the words "Applied Mathematics" then all references to this subject would be changed to "Applied Mathematics and Frisbology" including, for example, first year courses in Applied Mathematics and we suppose that this is not the intention.

Suppose further that the new Professor of Frisbology has been appointed before the actual changes have been made to the Calendar and that he feels that the title is not sufficiently imposing and persuades Senate to change the title of his Chair to "The Chair of Metastable Frisbodynamics". As a user of a

6

text replacement macro system we have two alternatives. Either we can scrap the old instruction to the system and write a new one to replace "Chair of Applied Mathematics" by "Chairs of Applied Mathematics and Metastable Frisbodynamics" or else, with some macro processors, we can write an extra macro which simply replaces "Frisbology" by "Metastable Frisbodynamics". This second solution makes two assumptions. Firstly it assumes that the word "Frisbology" is not to remain unchanged if it appears elsewhere in the text and in the case of the St Andrews Calendar this is a reasonable assumption. Secondly, and more important, it assumes that the replacement of the replaced text is itself scanned for further substitution. Some macro processors do this and others do not and this is a distinction we will refer to in other chapters of this book. If repeated scanning is permitted we must take care not to get into a recursive situation. Had the new Professor been slightly less title conscious he might have changed his title to Professor of Metastable Frisbology with disastrous recursive effects.

The above example was concerned simply with text replacement and both the text to be replaced and the replacement text itself consisted of a fixed sequence of letters and spaces. Frequently the context in which text to be replaced occurs is important and here conditional assembly of the replacement text is necessary. For example, code to be generated in assembly language will frequently depend on the type of parameters used and therefore some means of varying the corresponding code to be generated must be incorporated in the macro processor.

These ideas will be developed in subsequent chapters.

1.2 *Definitions*

As with so many other computer science topics, macro processing having developed on a broad front, has associated with it a wide range of technical terms, many of which are defined differently by different authors and others of which duplicate

one another. To be consistent within this book we give our
definition of the terminology to be used. Some of these definitions should be given in parallel but since books are most-
ly written and read serially it may be necessary to jump forwards and backwards to fully understand them on a first reading.

   Macro definition: a macro definition consists of a macro
template followed by a corresponding macro body. A macro definition is usually preceded by (that is, its template is usually preceded by) a special marker followed by a unique keyword,
for example $MACRODEF; similarly it is usually terminated by
the same symbol and another unique keyword, for example $MACRO-
END. The format for a typical macro definition is therefore

```
$MACRODEF
macro template
macro body
$MACROEND
```

   Macro template: a string of characters interspersed by
special markers which denote the formal arguments or parameters
of the macros. The macro template determines a skeleton against
which other character strings may be matched at macro expansion
time. The matching string would contain actual parameters which
replace the formal parameters in the corresponding macro body.
The complexity of the actual parameters allowed varies between
different macro processors and much of the power of a macro processor depends on the type of actual parameters permitted. We
will refer to this point from time to time throughout this book.
Note that a particular template may have no formal parameters.
This occurs for example when a simple substitution is to be
made.

   Many authors refer to the macro template as the macro
name but this terminology does not emphasise the importance of

the formal parameters. The implication of a template is that it has a well defined structure with "holes" into which the actual parameters will be inserted at macro expansion time. When there is no ambiguity we will occasionally refer to the macro template as the macro name.

As an example, a one address assembler may be made to look like a three address assembler by the introduction of a set of macros one of which could have template

SUM $1, $2, $3

where $1, $2 refer to the variables whose values are to be added and $3 indicates the name of the variable where the result is to be stored. Note that in this example the two commas are part of the template and need to be matched at macro expansion time. We will develop this definition a little later.

Macro body: a string of characters following a macro template. This string of characters determines the output at macro expansion time. In its simplest form the macro body may be output unchanged thus replacing the macro call at expansion time but frequently the process is more complicated than this. The macro body will usually contain formal parameters which will be replaced by actual parameters at expansion time and may also contain conditional code which will determine the output dependent on the actual parameters and possibly other information. In more sophisticated systems the macro body may itself contain macro calls or even new macro definitions.

For example, the macro body corresponding to the template

SUM $1, $2, $3

could be

FETCH $1

```
ADD     $2
STORE   $3
```

and at macro expansion time the call

```
SUM P, Q, R
```

would produce the output

```
FETCH P
ADD   Q
STORE R.
```

Suppose now that we want to add three numbers A, B, C together and to store the result in D. We could, and if the system permits it, should, define a new macro to do this but let us be stupid for the moment and use only the macro we have already defined. We could write

```
SUM A, B, D
SUM D, C, D
```

which would produce the output

```
FETCH   A
ADD     B
STORE   D
FETCH   D
ADD     C
STORE   D
```

which would inefficiently produce the right result. Assuming that our one address machine uses an accumulator which we will call ACC we could write a conditional macro as follows

```
$MACRODEF
SUM $1, $2, $3
IF $1 ≡ ACC SKIP
FETCH $1
ADD   $2
IF $3 ≡ ACC SKIP
STORE $3
$MACROEND
```

We introduce here a conditional IF...SKIP statement which we take to mean that if the condition holds then the next line is skipped. The condition is the literal equivalence of the two actual parameters. Note that at macro expansion time these parameters do not have any values so only literal equivalence is meaningful.

The pair of macro calls

```
SUM A, B, ACC
SUM ACC, C, D
```

would now produce the more acceptable code

```
FETCH A
ADD   B
ADD   C
STORE D.
```

If we required to add three numbers frequently we would of course define a separate macro to do this directly.

Macro call: formally this is an input string to be matched against a previously defined macro template. The effect of a macro call is to cause the macro processor to produce output text which replaces the call.

Macro expansion time: the time between the recognition

of a valid macro call and the completion of output of the corresponding text. This time includes that taken to execute conditional code, expand nested macro calls or to define internal macros contained in the corresponding macro body.

Nested macro call: a macro call which is internal to another macro body. As an example of a nested macro call which is internal to another macro call we could use the SUM macro defined above to extend to complex arithmetic.

```
$MACRODEF
COMPLEX SUM A, B, C
SUM A, B, C
SUM A+1, B+1, C+1
$MACROEND
```

where we are assuming that two consecutive locations have been set aside for the real and imaginary parts of A, B, C respectively and that, for example, A+1 refers to the machine location adjacent to A. In some macro systems recursive macro calls are allowed.

1.3 Some general concepts

The syntax of macro calls varies very widely. In our early example of text replacement we had the more general case in which every word of the text was considered as a candidate for replacement. We scanned the whole text looking for the phrase "Professor of Applied Mathematics" and so every word had to be inspected. Sometimes, for example if the phrase "Professor of Applied Mechanics" appeared in the text, we would get quite a long way before a mismatch occurred. Usually however the mismatch would be obvious in the first few letters. Nevertheless this is a time consuming method and if the generality of this example is not required then alternative methods are desirable.

12

When using macros associated with assemblers it is common to use the same field as the operator field for macro names. This reduces the number of characters which have to be scanned when attempting to match macros but there may still be a lot of failures particularly if there is an extensive collection of assembly language operation code mnemonics. The amount of scanning is often reduced by insisting that a special character, for example §, is used as the first character of a macro name and this character is not used to start any other operation code. This idea is also used in some general purpose macro processors. In this case greater generality is assured if it is possible for the user to change this reserved character by some declarative statement.

The method of terminating a macro name is also important and varies with different processors and the purpose for which they are being used. Suppose for example we were wanting to change the name Heath to Wilson wherever it occurred in a piece of text. If we simply looked for five consecutive characters H E A T H then if our text was about development of the tourist industry in the Scottish Highlands we would change any occurrence of heather to wilsoner. Even if we looked for a capital H to commence the sequence it would still be possible for the word heather to start a sentence with the same unfortunate result. If however we insisted upon the opening letter being a capital H and added a sixth character which could be either a space or a punctuation mark then we would overcome the problem unless the noun "heath" started a sentence. The macro name recognition technique is therefore very dependent upon the context in which the macro generator is being used. Notice that according to our definitions in Section 1.2 in the example above 'Heath' is the macro template, 'Wilson' is the macro body and the whole macro is of the parameterless type.

The use of macro calls in the operation field part of an assembler instruction is an example of a *restricted scope* macro.

Only the instruction field part is scanned for possible macro calls. In some general purpose macro generators it is possible to modify the scope of macro calls, either *statically* before scanning commences or *dynamically* in course of the scanning process. Such a scope restriction reduces the amount of scanning to be done.

There are several problems associated with the arguments of macros. First of all we have to determine how the arguments are to be identified both at macro definition and macro call time and this in turn raises the question of how the arguments are to be separated.

In the case of an assembler type macro processor the problem is easily solved by using the same method as for the base assembler. This either involves fixed fields with all the arguments lying in one field and separated from each other by commas or some other symbol or in the case of free input it is usual for at least the simplest type of argument to be in some definite position relative to the operation code. Thus with a free format macro

        OP A, B, C, D

the space between OP and A is a necessary delimiter and so also are the commas between the arguments A to D. D is either terminated by a space or by the end of a line (or card). In this context the characters space and comma have a special meaning and their general use is therefore restricted. If in the above example the line of code

        OP A, B, C, D

is the macro template then

        OP P,Q,R,S

would be a typical macro call in which case the actual parameters P,Q,R,S replace the formal parameters A,B,C,D respectively at macro expansion time. It may happen that on some
occasions some of the parameters are not required in a particular macro call. Thus in the above example if B is not required, then since the relative order of the parameters is
significant a suitable macro call would be of the type

OP P,,R,S

with the double comma indicating a missing parameter. Similarly if neither the A nor B parameters were required we might
write

OP ,,R,S

with obvious if clumsy meaning. Usually, by convention, a macro
call

OP P,Q,R

would associate P,Q,R with A,B,C respectively and assume that D
was not required.

Even in the simple case of assembler macro processors we
still have a problem and that is the recognition of the formal
parameters within the macro body. For a flexible system these
should be allowed to appear anywhere in the text of the macro
body and clearly if we simply use names such as A,B,C,D these
may also appear naturally in the macro body with other meanings.
It would be unnecessarily restrictive and confusing to insist
that these names must not be used with any other meaning and so
the simple solution of using a special marker to start formal
parameters is frequently used.

Thus it would be more usual to write

OP §A, §B, §C, §D

for a macro template and to use §A and so on for the formal
parameters throughout the macro body. Provided that § is an
excluded character except in this context there is no longer
any possibility of ambiguity. The separating commas would
appear to be redundant and so they are at macro definition
time but they are still required at macro call time. The
actual parameters at macro call time should still be as general
as possible since once they have been recognised immediately
following the macro name they are simply substituted as character strings for each occurrence of the corresponding formal
parameter within the macro body.

Macro processors which have a less rigid template format
than that of assemblers almost invariably use special markers
to indicate formal parameters. For example, if we wished to
make the macro

    ADD §A,§B,§C

more readable to the non-programming public we might use a template

    ADD §A TO §B WITH RESULT §C

and a corresponding call

    ADD X TO Y WITH RESULT C

To ensure absolute unambiguity the same, or some other
symbol is sometimes used to both start and terminate each formal parameter. Thus, for example, the above template could be
written

16

but with the same call as before.

We soon find that the restriction of call time parameters to simple variables or simple character strings is both tedious and undesirable. The first obvious development is to allow lists of variables but we then have to define exactly how the macro processor will handle such lists. For example we could simplify the macro to add a variable number of values together and form their result if we could write

    SUM §A TO §B

where §A is a list and §B is a simple variable and the macro body is written to sum the values in list §A and put the result in §B. A common way of handling the recognition of the list §A at run time is to enclose it in parentheses with some marker, often a comma, separating items in the list. Thus

    SUM (R,S,T,U,V) TO X

would be a possible call and

    SUM (A,B,C) TO T

would be another. Here either rigid syntax rules must be imposed or else the macro body must be carefully written to handle all possible cases that can arise.

If, for example, a user writes

    SUM (A,B,C) TO (X,Y)

the macro body must be able to handle this either by rejecting it, storing the result to X only or copying the result to both

X and Y or some other solution. In any case it must be possible for the user to deduce exactly what will happen. Special facilities are required to handle cases like this and we discuss them in more detail in later chapters.

Other facilities for handling parameters will be discussed in later chapters but this perhaps is the time to give a word of warning. It is easy to become obsessed with the tricks of a programming system and to look for "tricky" solutions to problems. This is undesirable since apart from being time wasting it also makes debugging and even just understanding difficult for other users. There is a great difference between tricky and elegant solutions. For example the use of recursion in evaluating factorials is tricky (and a lot more besides) whereas the use of recursion in the Towers of Hanoi problem described in chapter 3 is elegant.

1.4 *Summary*

The use of macro processors has developed since the early days of programming starting with very simple text replacement facilities usually in conjunction with assembler language programs. In subsequent chapters several different macro processing systems will be described, some of these being special purpose and others more general purpose. The reason for the existence of so many different macro processors is partly because the subject has developed rapidly over the last decade and many authors have worked in parallel but mainly because different subject areas require different facilities and no one has yet produced or is likely to produce a universal system which is both useful and efficient.

There is a real danger in a book like this developing into a shopping list of available products. We will attempt in each chapter not only to describe the actual systems but also to assess the objectives of the system and the extent to which these have been met.

18

One final point which cannot be emphasised too strongly. Because of the syntax of many macro calls there is a danger of confusing the idea of macros with that of subroutine or procedure calls. If the confusion is not already in your mind then ignore the rest of this paragraph! A macro generator is briefly a text replacement system and after macro replacement time no trace of the original macro call exists in the text. The macro body is not "executed" at macro expansion time. It merely replaces, after substitution of the revelant parameters, the actual macro call. A subroutine or procedure call on the other hand is replaced at compilation time by a link to a fixed routine and parameters are usually only passed at run time. The uses of macro processors and of procedures are quite different as we will see in subsequent chapters.

1.5 *Bibliography*

The few references mentioned here are of an introductory or general nature. More specialised references are given in later chapters. The most comprehensive single contribution is the survey article by P.J. Brown and this can be read with profit both now and again later after reading further in this book.

Brown, P.J. A survey of macro processors; pp. 77-88. *Annual Review in Automatic Programming*, vol. 6. Pergamon Press, 1969.

Greenwald, I. A technique for handling macro instructions; pp. 21-2. *Comm. A.C.M.* 2(1), Nov. 1959.

McIlroy, M.D. Macro instruction extensions of compiler languages; pp. 214-20. *Comm. A.C.M.* 3(4), April 1960.

Wegner, P. *Programming languages, information structures, and machine organisation*; pp. 145-227. McGraw-Hill, 1968.

Gries, D. *Compiler construction for digital computers*, pp. 413-34. Wiley, 1971.

2 · Assembler language macro processing

2.1 *Introduction*

Near the beginning of chapter 1 we indicated that the
origin of macro processors was in connection with assembler
language programming. Initially the intention was very simple,
namely to allow fairly standard pieces of code to be inserted
within some assembler coding by the use of an identifying name
with or without parameters. The same run time effect could
have been obtained by the use of a subroutine or procedure
call but the intention was to avoid time consuming linkage and
passing of parameters. Since the parameters were inserted
directly into the code at macro expansion time no run time substitution of parameters was involved. Macro instructions were
written along with the normal one-one assembler code instructions providing an extension to the language. The extension
was no longer one-one but differed from high level languages in
that the assembler language programmer knew exactly what code
was generated by his program and was not dependent on the hidden inner working of a compiler to produce his machine code.
At that period compilers were less logically defined and constructed and the restrictions on the use of high level language statements built up into both formidable and annoying
proportions.

The use of macros provides a number of additional benefits to the assembler language programmer. The coding effort
is reduced since problem oriented sets of macros can be produced and then used by all the members of a group working in
that problem area. If the important macros are written by

more experienced programmers, less highly trained juniors can be used in the team without significantly lowering the overall standard. The amount of detailed thinking by all but the writers of the macro bodies is also reduced. The code produced should in general be more efficient than independently written assembly code and since the macro bodies can be fully tested independently the debugging problems should be lessened. In addition the volume of written rather than executable code is considerably reduced and this also makes debugging somewhat simpler. By insisting on the use of macros in certain conditions standardised coding conventions may be more readily enforced and interfaces can be more efficiently standardised.

2.2 A choice of assembler language

In order to illustrate the concepts of macro processing in assembler languages it is necessary to define an assembler language itself. It would be possible to define here a theoretical assembler but there is little value in defining yet another. Since the author is most familiar with IBM 360 Assembler Language (IBM, Form C28-6514) this language will be used for illustrative purposes. Only a small subset of the language will be needed. A much more detailed and very readable account of the IBM 360 assembly language can be found in Struble (1969).

In order to understand the code generated, the following basic details of IBM 360 architecture are required. The main store is byte oriented with each byte being addressable. Bytes may be built up into half, full or double length words of two, four or eight bytes respectively. In addition to main storage there is a set of 16 general purpose registers each consisting of four bytes. Their addresses are 0 to 15. There are also four floating point registers each of eight bytes in length but we will not be concerned with these here.

The machine language instructions fall into five basic types which are characterised by their addressing structure, that is by whether operands are in registers, main store or in the instruction itself and further, in the case of main store operands, whether addressing is by base and displacement or by base, index and displacement.

The simplest instruction is of the register to register (RR) type. The instruction occupies two bytes of storage and a typical instruction of this sort would be

    LR   R1,R2

where LR is the operation code part and R1,R2 specify particular general purpose registers. The effect of this instruction is to load register R1 with the contents of register R2. Another instruction of this type is

    LTR   R1,R2

and is exactly the same as LR except that it also sets a condition code which can be subsequently tested.

The next group of instructions are of the register to main storage (RX) type. These instructions each occupy four bytes of storage and a typical example is

    L   R1,D2(X2,B2)

which is an instruction to load register R1 with the contents of four consecutive bytes of main storage, the leftmost byte of this quadruple having address obtained by adding the address of the displacement D2 to the address of the index register X2 and the base register B2.

One other RX instruction which we will require is

    A R1, S2

which adds the contents of registers R1 and the main store full word with address S2 and stores the result in R1. S2 of course can be of the form D2(X2,B2) as before.

There are two other instructions needed, both of which are RX instructions but look like unorthodox one address instructions.

These are

B S2

and

BZ S2

and are both part of the extended instruction set. These are instructions which are good mnemonics and expand to a less readable but basic instruction by use of a system macro.

B S2

is an unconditional branch to main store location S2 and expands to

BC 15, S2

which is a branch on condition type of instruction.

BZ S2

is a branch on condition code zero and expands to

BC 8, S2

In both cases S2 can again be of the form D2(X2,B2).

The RS instructions also occupy four bytes of storage but have three operands instead of two as in the RX instructions. For example, the load multiple instruction

    LM R1, R2, D2(B2)

which loads consecutive registers from R1 to R2 inclusive with the information in main store commencing at the byte addressed by the displacement D2 modified by the base register B2. If the number of register R2 is less than that of register R1 then the consecutive registers from R1 to 15 followed by registers from 0 to R2 are similarly loaded.

The store immediate (SI) type of instruction also occupies four bytes of storage. Their effect is to use the actual data specified in the instruction in some way. For example, the instruction

    MVI D1(B1),I2

moves the actual byte of data symbolised here by the name I2 into the main store location addressed by the displacement D1 modified by the base register B1.

Finally, store to store (SS) instructions occupy six bytes of storage and as their type suggests they operate on two main store addresses. For example, the instruction

    MVC D1(L,B1), D2(B2)

moves the string of characters of length L beginning at the main store location whose address is given by the displacement D2 modified by the base register B2 to the string of consecutive bytes starting at the address given by the displacement D1 modified by the base register B1. The only condition on the value of L is that it must lie between 1 and 256.

A single assembly language statement is written in a standard format. Each statement has four fields namely label, operation, operands and remarks each being variable in length and separated from the others by blanks. Since the label field is optional it is necessary to impose the further conditions that if a label is present it must commence in column 1. If column 1 is blank it is assumed that no label exists for that statement and the first non-blank field is the operation code. Apart from these conditions instructions are in free format. A macro call can be initiated by placing the macro name in the operation field and so a distinguishing symbol is required to identify such a call.

In addition to the assembly language equivalents of the five machine code operation types discussed above there are also assembler declarative statements which enable symbols and data to be defined. For example,

```
LABEL DC F'202'
```

defines a fixed point, four byte long constant with value 202 and name "LABEL" by which it can be referred to later in the program. Various other data types are available and will be defined as they are required.

One may also define symbols and the corresponding work space without assigning values by, for example, the use of the statement

```
LABEL   DS   F
```

which reserves one four byte fixed point constant with name "LABEL". Furthermore the declarative statement

```
LIST   DS   18F
```

reserves a list of 18 four byte fixed point constants.

The statement

LABEL EQU EXPRESSION

enables an expression to be associated with a name.

With this brief introduction to 360 assembly language we are now in a position to develop the ideas of the use of macros in this environment.

2.3 *Macro definition*

In the IBM 360 macro assembler system the general form of a macro definition is as follows

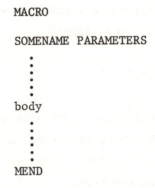

MACRO

SOMENAME PARAMETERS

.
.
.
.

body

.
.
.
.

MEND

The words MACRO and MEND act as brackets around this macro definition. Macro definition inside a macro definition is not permitted so there are no problems concerning the scope of a definition to be resolved. All macro definitions which are not catalogued in the main macro library must appear at the head of the program in which they are to be used and once declared they are immediately available for use.

The second line of the macro definition behaves like the macro template defined in chapter 1. It is however a very simple form of a template. The name of the macro is immediately determined since it appears in the name field of the line of code. The parameters may be quite complicated and we will discuss them in more detail later. We will only mention here that if the macro has no parameters then the parameter list field is left blank.

Between the template line and the closing bracket MEND appears the macro body. This is the text which, after substitution of parameters, if any, will be copied into the source text in place of the actual macro call. Once defined, a macro may be used as often as desired in the calling program. It is also permitted to have macro calls in the body of a macro definition. Such a call is referred to as an *inner macro* call. It is important to know that in the IBM 360 Assembler Macro System the substitution of inner macro call text is not done at declaration time of the outer macro body but is done on each and every call encountered at macro expansion time of the outer macro from the main program. This leads to inefficiencies at macro expansion time but this is offset to some extent by the reduction in the volume of code to be held in the macro library and also allows the definition of inner macro calls in library macros to be delayed until expansion time thus increasing the flexibility of the system. A decision of this type is a design decision and clearly therefore considerable thought should be given by the designer before making it. An alternative solution would have been to give the user the option of expanding inner macro calls at definition time but this may lead to confusion particularly when a team is working on some project.

2.4   *Simple parameters*

Parameters have to be recognised not only in the macro template but also in the macro body. In the macro body a parameter can appear anywhere and does not even have to take up a whole subfield. Examples of this will be given shortly but as a consequence it is necessary that the formal parameters of a macro must be uniquely recognisable. This is done by prefixing every formal parameter with an ampersand (&). This is only necessary at macro definition time. The actual parameters used at macro expansion time can be easily matched with the formal parameters and, in general, one does not wish these actual parameters to begin with an ampersand although there is no good reason why they should not. To the macro expansion routine the actual parameters are just character strings to be substituted for every occurrence of the formal parameters in the macro body. A further arbitrary restriction on the formal parameters is that the ampersand must be followed by from 1 to 7 letters or digits.

The formal parameters are declared in the template by listing them after the macro name with at least one blank between the name and the first formal parameter, the various parameters being separated by commas and the list terminated by a blank.

An example is

        LANDT &REG, &ITEM, &COND, &TO

where LANDT is the macro name and &REG, &ITEM, &COND and &TO is the formal parameter list. It is also permitted to include one formal parameter before the macro name in the label field. In fact any of the other parameters may be used as labels too so strictly speaking it is not necessary to have a special parameter for this purpose but it is useful as a reminder if one also wishes, for example, to put a label on the first line of the macro body code.

For our first complete example of a macro we take

```
            MACRO
&HERE       LANDT       &REG, &ITEM, &COND, &TO
```

```
&HERE      L          &REG, &ITEM,
           LTR        &REG, &REG
           B&COND     &TO
           MEND
```

A subsequent macro call

```
ICI   LANDT   3, LA, Z, VA
```

produces the code

```
+ ICI  L  3,  LA
+         LTR,  3,3
+         BZ VA
```

There are one or two points to notice here. Firstly
each line of code produced is preceded by a + sign. This is
a convention to indicate in the program listing that a macro
expansion has been made at this point and is not really part
of the code generated. The assembler ignores this + sign.
The label ICI appears on the first line of code because the
formal parameter &HERE appears in this place in the macro body.
Exactly the same effect could have been obtained by declaring
the macro template as

```
LANDT  &REG, &ITEM, &COND, &TO &HERE
```

and making the call

```
LANDT  3, LA, Z, VA, ICI
```

The use of &REG and &ITEM is fairly obvious but it should
be noted that &COND is used as only part of the operation field
for a conditional branch instruction. The effect of this piece

of program is to load a register from main store, set a conditional code with the LTR instruction and branch on zero to the label VA which is assumed to be declared elsewhere in the program.

It should be remembered that macro calls follow the same convention as assembler instructions. That is, if a label is present it must start in column 1 and if not, then the macro name must not start before column 2 with column 1 left blank.

Another call on this macro might be

```
HERE   LANDT  4,THERE,,GO
```

which would generate the code

```
+    HERE   L     4,THERE
+           LTR   4,4
+           B     GO
```

including the final unconditional branch. This is because the actual parameter corresponding to the formal parameter &TO is null.

2.5   *Keyword parameters*

The formal parameters used above are matched against the actual parameters according to their relative position in the template. Frequently there are obvious default options for the actual parameter names and it is useful if these can be assumed automatically as default options. This however would cause difficulties with the matching of the actual and formal parameter lists. To overcome this problem and at the same time to remove the implied ordering of parameters the idea of *keyword parameters* is introduced.

These are declared in the template by writing an equal sign (=) after the formal parameter name. The default value

can then be specified if desired by writing it immediately
after the equal sign. If the field after the equal sign is
left empty then the default option is null.

For example

```
MACRO
MOVE     &FROM=, &TO=, &LNTH=80
MVC      &TO.(&LNTH), &FROM
MEND
```

followed by the macro call

```
MOVE     FROM=HERE, TO=THERE, LNTH=100
```

would produce the code

```
+      MVC THERE(100),HERE
```

which moves 100 characters from HERE to THERE. Note that at
call time the keywords are used without ampersands. Although
in this example they have been used in the same order as the
template this is not necessary.

Thus

```
MOVE  LNTH=100, TO=THERE, FROM=HERE
```

would produce the same code. We have slipped in here one extra idea without previously defining it. Following the use of
&TO in the macro body there appears a period (.) which dis-
appears in the output code. The purpose of the period is to
indicate the end of the formal parameter &TO when this does not
coincide with an obvious end of field. To avoid ambiguity, a
period indicates the end of the formal parameter and implies
the concatenation of the string so far with whatever follows.

In an earlier example in which we used the sequence

    B&COND

it was not necessary to use a period between B and & to indicate concatenation since & uniquely identified the following
formal parameter. Some systems avoid this problem by both
starting and terminating formal parameters with some special
character such as the ampersand.

   Notice that the macro call

    MOVE TO=THERE, FROM=HERE

produces the code

    +   MVC THERE(80),HERE

the value 80 being provided by default.

   To conclude this section we note that simple and keyword
parameters may both be used in the same template. The simple
parameters must always precede the keyword ones since simple
parameters must always be present whereas keyword parameters
are optional.

2.6   *Parameter lists*

   When simple parameters only are being used the number of
parameters used at call time, even if some have implied null
value, must match exactly the number of parameters declared in
the template. Similarly, when using keyword parameters the
total number used at call time cannot exceed the total number
declared in the template. This is very soon found to be an
annoying restriction and also reduces the usefulness of the
system. To overcome this difficulty a system function called
&SYSLIST is introduced. A subscript on &SYSLIST, for example

32

&SYSLIST(4), specifies the particular parameter in the macro expansion time parameter list that is to be used. If one could only use integer constants as subscripts there would be no advantage in using this notation since the parameter list would be limited by the maximum subscript specified but it is possible to use an integer variable as a subscript with various values given to the variable at macro expansion time. This technique will be described in the next section.

2.7 *Conditional assembly*

So far we have thought of the macro body as consisting of text to be copied directly to the output stream together with instances of formal parameters which will be replaced by actual parameters at expansion time. There are many occasions when it is desirable to be able to vary the output depending on some internal conditions at expansion time. Thus we may sometimes wish to omit certain statements or to choose one of several alternative statements or even to iterate a collection of statements until some condition, for example completion of the scanning of the parameter list, is complete. Note that these are not final program loops but are purely macro expansion time loops.

To meet this requirement we introduce an internal language which is independent of the language being generated (in this case 360 Assembler Language) which controls the flow of code generation inside the macro. We need to be able to label *internally*, lines of the macro body including the conditional statements themselves. When these labels are attached to lines of code which are not themselves conditional statements their function is to assist control of flow at expansion time and they are not to be passed to the output stream. Such labels are distinguished by a starting period (.) followed by 1 to 7 letters or digits of which the first must be a letter. They are called sequence symbols. It should be emphasised that these labels are purely local and never appear in the code generated by the macro call. There is no confusion with the previous use of the period since it is the first character of the label and there is no implied concatenation.

There are two very simple branching instructions with operator mnemonics AGO and AIF. AGO is an unconditional branch and has format

optional sequence symbol   AGO   sequence symbol

For example,

.L1   AGO   .L2

or

AGO   .NEXT

both with obvious meanings.

The operation AIF has format

optional sequence symbol AIF (logical expression) sequence symbol

For example,

AIF   ('&ANS' EQ '').DONE

tests for a null parameter. The quotation marks imply that the actual parameter corresponding to &ANS is to be compared literally with the null string and if they are identical then a branch is to be made to the statement with sequence symbol .DONE. Otherwise macro expansion continues sequentially. The logical expression may be quite complicated including logical connectives AND, OR and NOT and the relational operators EQ,

NE, LT, LE, GT and GE with the usual meaning and syntax. The logical expression must evaluate to either TRUE or FALSE at macro expansion time.

A simple example is as follows

```
           MACRO
           ADD     &A, &B, &RESULT
           AIF     ('&A' EQ").NOLOAD
           L       1,&A
.NOLOAD    A       1,&B
           AIF     ('&RESULT' EQ").DONE
           ST      1,&RESULT
.DONE      MEND
```

The macro call

```
           ADD X,Y,Z
```

produces the code

```
    +      L     1,X
    +      A     1,Y
    +      ST    1,Z
```

whereas

```
           ADD X,Y
```

produces

```
    +      L     1,X
    +      A     1,Y
```

since the actual value of &RESULT is assumed to be null. The pair of calls

```
ADD P,Q
ADD ,R,S
```

produces the code

```
+       L    1,P
+       A    1,Q
+       A    1,R
+       ST   1,S
```

thus allowing a degree of optimisation.

If a branch is to be made conditionally to a statement which already has its own label then a sequence symbol cannot be used. This problem is overcome by introducing a *no operation* statement which has the form

```
sequence symbol    ANOP
```

and which can be inserted anywhere in the macro body.

These conditional assembly statements would be fairly weak if they could only compare literal strings in the logical expression part. It must be remembered that none of the actual parameters have explicit values at macro expansion time. There are however various system functions which can be used and also variables which can be declared and utilised at macro expansion time only.

We have already mentioned the system function &SYSLIST in section 2.6. Apart from referencing the parameters in the macro call by, for example, the notation &SYSLIST(1) we can also determine how many parameters there are by the *attribute reference* N'&SYSLIST which returns as its value the number of parameters in the current macro call. There are a number of other

attribute references (that is, built in functions) and we will
describe some of these later.

To establish a simple loop operation inside a macro body
we need some local count variables. The simplest of these,
which is strictly local to the macro body in which it is declared, is the local arithmetic variable. This is declared in
the macro in which it is used by a statement.

      LCLA   symbol name list

where *symbol name* satisfies the same rules as a formal parameter (that is, it commences with an ampersand followed by
from 1 to 7 letters or digits) and the list looks like a formal parameter list. The use of LCLA not only declares the
names of a local arithmetic variable but also sets its initial
value to 0. There is no choice of initial value here but this
is no disadvantage since such variables are used mainly for
counting. Arithmetic on local variables is carried out by the
SETA instruction. This has format

      name of SETA symbol   SETA   arithmetic expression.

For example

```
          LCLA     &J
&J        SETA     &J+1
```

declares a local variable &J and increments its value by 1.

We can now give a simple example of a macro which at expansion time has a looping operation.

```
            MACRO
            SUM
            LCLA      &I
   &I       SETA      &I+2
            L         &SYSLIST(1),&SYSLIST(2)
   .LOOP    ANOP
   &I       SETA      &I+1
            AIF       (&I EQ N'&SYSLIST).STORE
            A         &SYSLIST(1), &SYSLIST(&I)
            AGO       .LOOP
   .STORE   AIF       ('&SYSLIST(&I)'EQ'').DONE
            ST        &SYSLIST(1),&SYSLIST(&I)
   .DONE    MEND
```

A macro call

        SUM   1,A,B,C,D,X

would produce the code

```
   +        L     1,A
   +        A     1,B
   +        A     1,C
   +        A     1,D
   +        ST    1,X
```

whereas

        SUM   3,P,Q,R,

would produce the code

```
   +        L     3,P
   +        A     3,Q
```

2.8   *Conditional assembly data types*

There are three basic data types corresponding to arithmetic, boolean and character variables. These can either be entirely local to the macro in which they are declared and do not have an existence outside that macro or they can be passed from one macro to another in which case they exist in a global sense, at least at macro expansion time.

We have already had an example of a local variable. A local arithmetic variable was declared with the operator LCLA and arithmetic was carried out on it with the operator SETA. Similarly there are boolean and character declarations with operator mnemonics LCLB and LCLC respectively and associated assignment operators SETB and SETC. The initial value for a local boolean variable is FALSE and the initial value for a character variable is the null string.

If we wish to pass values of variables between macros, and this includes passing information to inner macros, it is necessary to declare the variable as being *global* in all of the macros which need to use it. This is done in the same way as for local variables but with the operator mnemonics GBLA, GBLB and GBLC. The assignment mnemonics SETA, SETB and SETC can be used with both local and global variables. It must be emphasised here that a global variable is only available to macros which explicitly declare it as global. An inner macro which does not declare a particular variable as global may well use the same name for a local variable which will then be completely independent of any other use of that variable.

A powerful feature of the 360 macro assembler is the ability to structure data into lists. We have already seen that the arguments of a macro call can be regarded as a list and referenced by the system function &SYSLIST. Each argument may also be a list of elements enclosed in round brackets. Further it is possible to declare both local and global variables as one dimensional arrays. This is done by declaring the array in a "LCL" or "GBL" declaration with the size of array needed being declared as an integer in brackets after the variable name. For example,

```
LCLA     &I(20)
```

declares an arithmetic array &I with twenty elements subscripted from 1 to 20 and being referenced within the macro body in the usual way. Thus &I(6) refers to the sixth element of the array. A subscript may be appended to a variable in any context so, in particular, subscripts on subscripts to any depth are allowed.

The attribute reference function N'&L returns a value equal to the number of elements on the list &L at the current time. This can be used to produce declarations of, for example, lists of full word constants, each with a unique name as follows

```
            MACRO
            FCONST      &F
            LCLA        &I
.F          ANOP
&I          SETA        &I+1
F&F(&I)     DC          F'&F(&I)'
            AIF         (&I LT N'&F).F
            MEND
```

A macro call

```
FCONST  (100,120,180,260)
```

will produce the output

+	F100	DC	F'100'
+	F120	DC	F'120'
+	F180	DC	F'180'
+	F260	DC	F'260'

thus reducing the tedium of writing assembler programs.

A nice example of a simple automatic register management technique has been given by Kent (1969). The idea is to keep a current list of the names of main store variables which have been loaded into registers so that a register load operation from main store has only to be carried out whenever the required variable is not already in a register. If it *is* in a register, but not the specified one, then a register to register operation is carried out. Care has to be taken to ensure that the code being generated can only be entered from the start since it must be remembered that this optimisation is being carried out at macro expansion time and the code is not used until run time.

The full macro, which is given in fig. 2.1 (see page 42) is in two parts. The first part checks to see if the required item is already in the specified register. If so it simply exits without generating any code. The use of the command MEXIT causes a return to the calling statement. The second part searches the list &INREGS to see if the item is already there. If so, knowing that it is not in the required register, we can output a register to register operation. Otherwise we output a main store to register load operation and in both of the last two cases we update the list &INREGS with the name of &ITEM in the appropriate place.

2.9 *Attributes*

We have already mentioned the attribute N' which when applied to a list returns the current number of elements in the list. In particular, this enabled us to find the length

```
1                      MACRO
2                      FETCH    &REG,&ITEM
3                      GBLC     &INREGS(15)
4                      LCLA     &I
5                      AIF      ('&INREGS(&REG)'  NE  '&ITEM').SR
6                      MEXIT
7       .SRCH          AIF      (&I EQ 15).LOAD
8       &I             SETA     &I+1
9                      AIF      ('&INREGS(&I)'  NE  '&ITEM').SRCH
10                     LR       &REG,&I
11                     AGO      .MARK
12      .LOAD          L        &REG,&ITEM
13      .MARK          ANOP
14      &INREGS(&REG)  SETC     '&ITEM'
15                     MEND

16                     MACRO
17                     ADD      &X,&Y,&Z
18                     GBLC     &INREGS(15)
19                     FETCH    1,&X
20                     A        1,&Y
21                     ST       1,&Z
22      &INREGS(1)     SETC     '&Z'
23                     MEND
```

Fig. 2.1   Automatic register handling macro due to W. Kent.

of a particular variable length list being used as a parameter
to a macro. Similarly the attribute K' returns the number of
characters in the name of the corresponding variable.

Another useful attribute is the *type attribute* T'. This
returns as its value a single character corresponding to the
type of the identifier following it. For example, if &I is a
formal parameter of a macro and the corresponding actual parameter has been declared in the main program as a hexadecimal
constant then T'&I returns the literal value X. A list of
some other values of the type attribute is given in fig. 2.2.

A	A-type address constant.
B	Binary constant.
C	Character constant.
D	Long floating-point constant.
E	Short floating-point constant.
F	Full-word fixed-point constant.
H	Half-word fixed-point constant.
P	Packed decimal constant.
S	S-type address constant.
V	V-type address constant.
X	Hexadecimal constant.
Z	Zoned decimal constant.
I	Machine instruction.
J	Control section name.
M	Macro instruction.
T	External symbol.
W	CCW assembler instruction.

Fig. 2.2   Some sample values of the type attribute.

The *length attribute* L' returns as value the number of bytes occupied by the corresponding variable. The *integer* and *scaling* attributes I' and S' respectively return the number of digits in the integer and fractional parts of a variable. These are perhaps best illustrated by an example.

Suppose we have declared a packed decimal constant

```
NUMBER   DC   P'4.36'
```

and pass it to a macro as the actual value of a formal parameter .&PAR.   Then

```
K'&PAR
```

returns the value P since "NUMBER" is a packed decimal constant.

```
L'&PAR
```

returns the value 2 since the packed decimal constant occupies two bytes.

```
I'&PAR    and    S'&PAR
```

return the values 1 and 2 respectively since "NUMBER" has a one digit decimal part and two digit fractional part.

The availability of attributes clearly allows one to write much more flexible macros. For example, the macro for declaring constants described in Section 2.8 can be extended to cover a wide variety of constants of different types with perhaps one example being given in the main program and the rest generated automatically by the macro. The reader should try to write such a macro.

2.10 *System macros*

To further ease the task of the assembly language programmer, manufacturer supplied macros may be used to facilitate I/O operations and store management.

Thus OPEN and CLOSE macros are frequently available to prepare a data set for processing with all the trivial but tedious tasks associated with it. Similarly GET, PUT and CONTROL macros handle the input/output requirements with suitable precautions being taken to handle error conditions both logical and physical.

Similarly SAVE and RETURN macros can be used to handle subroutine linkage problems and most manufacturers supply a large number of such macros. There is little point in describing their full function here since they clearly vary depending on the hardware for which they are written. For further information the reader should consult the systems manuals at his own installation.

Another systems use of macros is in the simplification of Job Control Language sequences, particularly in cases in which a simple user requirement still demands a large number of job control instructions. Here a simple JCL macro such as ALGOL GO could be used by the casual and unsophisticated user to release into the system the sometimes staggeringly large number of job control statements required to compile and run a simple Algol job. Other grand names are sometimes given to this macro facility such as Catalogued Data Set Usage but basically it is still a simple macro facility with limited scope.

2.11 *Summary*

Macro processors have commonly been used as a means of extending the basic language available to assembly language programmers and at the same time reducing the coding effort and improving the uniformity of code written. The IBM 360 assembler macro system is a fairly typical example of an

assembler macro processor. Its main power is in the variety
of parameter types available, in its conditional instructions,
in its attribute functions and in the provision of local and
global variables for the transmission and accumulation of information at macro expansion time.

The macro recognition time overhead is reduced by putting
macro calls in a statement format with the macro name being in
the operation code field of an assembly instruction. System
macros which are manufacturer supplied with the system reduce
the coding effort in handling input/output and storage management functions. Similarly JCL macros can simplify the running
of jobs by unsophisticated and indeed any users.

2.12 *Bibliography*

Most manufacturers supply a macro processor in conjunction with their assembly language facilities. The reader should
consult his own installation library for further information.
Since this chapter has been based on the IBM 360 Assembler
Macro Processor reference is made to IBM literature. The book
by Struble is excellent as a model for assembly language texts
and contains some information on macros. The paper by Kent is
lucid and contains many useful tips on the use of macros, not
only for IBM users although clearly it is IBM system oriented.

Freeman, D.N. Macro language design for System/360; pp. 63-77,
    IBM Systems J. 5(2), 1966.

IBM OS/360 Assembler Language, Form C28-6514, IBM Corporation,
    Poughkeepsie, New York, 1966.

IBM OS/360 Supervisor and data management macro instructions,
    Form C28-6647, IBM Corporation, Poughkeepsie, New York,
    1966.

Kent, W. Assembler language macro processing: a tutorial
    oriented towards the IBM 360; pp. 183-96. *Computing
    Surveys*, vol. 1, no.4, December, 1969.

Struble, G. *Assembler language programming the IBM System/360.*
Addison Wesley, 1969.

2.13 *Examples*

(1) The macro CALL is defined by

```
MACRO
CALL     &SUBR, &LREG = R12
L        &LREG, = A(&SUBR)
BALR     R5, &LREG
MEND
```

Determine the effect of the macro calls

CALL SEEK, LREG = R9

and

CALL INDEX

(2) If your computer installation does not use the 360 Assembler Macro System find out what macro facilities are available. Compare these with the facilities outlined in this
chapter with particular reference to the way in which parameters can be used and also any equivalent facility to
attribute functions.

Rewrite all the macros discussed in this chapter in
any Assembly Language Processor which is available to you.

(3) The macros FCONST in section 2.8 produced lists of F type
"define constant" statements. Generalise this so that constants of any specified type can be handled in a similar
way.

(4) Write a macro MOVE which given an integer N, N main store addresses and another integer i will move the contents of those main store locations into consecutive registers from Ri. Your program should check that both N and i are in the acceptable range (in the case of the IBM 360 from 1 to 15) and should be able to handle the case in which the start register is different to R1 and there is a "wrap around" from R15 to R1.

(5) Write an assembler macro called TABLE with parameters TBLNAME, NEXTENT, MAXENT and a list of entries (ENT1, ENT2,..., ENTn) of equal length. NEXTENT is a pointer to the next free space and MAXENT indicates the maximum size of table permitted. The purpose of TABLE is to add the elements in the list to the table with name TBLNAME and to output a suitable message when the table is full.

Write another macro called LOOK with parameters TBLNAME, ITEM, POSTN, MAXENT which will return the position POSTN of ITEM in TBLNAME if it is there and a value 0 otherwise.

3 · String handling macro processors

3.1 *Introduction*

We describe three macro processors which are special purpose in the sense that they are stand alone and are particularly
efficient at string handling. They are however general purpose
in the sense that their application area is wide and they are
not aimed at the extension of a single language like an assembly language macro processor. The first processor we shall describe is TRAC (Text reckoning and compiling) which was designed and implemented by Mooers and Deutsch (1965). The system is
still in use and its devotees are very enthusiastic about its
capabilities although perhaps not quite so evangelic as APL
addicts.

Secondly we will describe GPM (General purpose macrogenerator) which was designed by Strachey (1965). Both TRAC and GPM
appeared at about the same time but were designed quite independently. Despite this they have many features in common although their implementation is quite different. They both have
the same aim in the sense that they are symbol string processors with both input and output being simply strings of symbols.
They are both powerful systems incorporating such features as
conditional expressions and recursive functions which are almost essential in this type of processor.

The third processor, ML/I, was designed and implemented by
Brown (1967) who was influenced by Strachey's work but whose
processor, at least externally, appears quite different to the
user. The processor is very flexible and can be used both in a
simple minded way by the casual user and in a sophisticated way

by the professional who is prepared to study its more complex features. ML/I was designed to be bootstrapped on to different computer systems and is in use in a lot of computing laboratories.

3.2 *A general description of TRAC*

The internal mechanism of TRAC involves scanning and possibly repeated scanning of input strings with corresponding evaluation of functions as full information for this evaluation becomes available. The system was designed to operate in a time sharing environment using a reactive typewriter terminal. It provides facilities for writing procedures for accepting, naming, storing and manipulating any character string and for treating any string of characters as an executable procedure or as a name or as executable text.

String manipulation languages require to provide facilities for the basic operation on strings such as:

accept as input any character or string of characters coming from the terminal.

Store characters or strings as text or literal or as normal strings after giving them a name.

Operate on them or emit them according to the application.

The flow of information inside TRAC can be represented diagrammatically as in fig. 3.1. This appears to be quite complicated but is in fact quite simple. The source text comes from the interactive typewriter and the object text returns there. The form store is the library of named strings or forms as they are called in TRAC which are built up by the user. The only complication is in how the scanning of strings and evaluation of procedures or functions is carried out. Basically all scanning is carried out from the active string with the function to be performed being built up on the neutral string.

90181

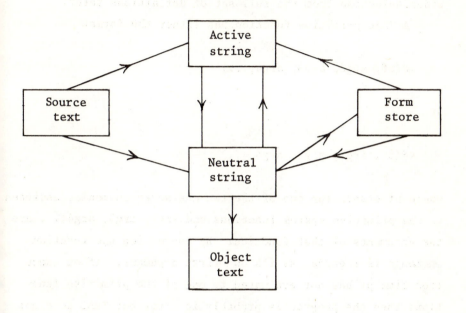

Fig. 3.1 Diagrammatic flow of information in TRAC

Once all the information for a particular function has been
built up on the neutral string the function is executed and its
result either stays on the neutral string or is returned to the
active string for further scanning. One special function acts
in a different way by outputting a selected part of the neutral
string and then deleting it from that string. It is the possibility of returning a string for further scanning and consequent
further evaluation of functions that makes TRAC so powerful.

TRAC contains a very limited number of primitive functions
which are part of the system and these primitive functions cannot be extended. This would appear to severely limit the power

of the system but this is not really so since procedures can
be built up in the form store and subsequently called for execution by the primitive call function.

We introduce first a few of the TRAC primitive functions
to further illustrate the basic concepts and will then give a
wider selection from the full set of definitions later.

A TRAC primitive function has either the format

#(pf, arg2, arg3, arg4,...)

or

##(pf, arg2, arg3, arg4,...)

where pf stands for one of the two character mnemonics assigned
to the primitive system functions and arg2, arg3, arg4,... are
the arguments of that function. By convention the function
mnemonic is regarded as its own first argument. If at execution time pf has not evaluated to one of the primitive functions then the program is probably in error but TRAC does not
terminate execution. It assumes that the programmer knows what
he is doing and returns a null result. Similarly if the wrong
number of arguments is given TRAC is very tolerant. If there
are too few arguments it supplies null values for the rest and
if there are too many it ignores the extra ones although it
does evaluate them first. This permits the user to program for
side effects of function evaluation if he wishes.

The symbols #(and ##(have two roles to play. Firstly
they both indicate during the scanning process that a function
follows and has eventually to be evaluated. Secondly they indicate whether the function is active or neutral. The characters #(indicate that an active function follows whereas ##(
indicates that a neutral function follows. The terminology
here is rather misleading since the function evaluation is

identical in both cases. The only difference is in what happens to the *result* of the function evaluation. In the case of the active function the result is passed back to the active string for rescanning whereas for a neutral function it is passed to the neutral string where it replaces the function call. In both cases the function call is deleted from the neutral string. It would have been better to call them active result function and neutral result function but this is rather clumsy. Every function in TRAC has a result although sometimes the result may be the null string. A function may also have an effect which is different from the result. For example there is a function which will store a form with a given name in the form store and this is its effect. Its result however is the null string. We will be careful to distinguish between effect and result when they are different in each of the functions that we define.

To avoid repetition we will show each of the functions to be defined in its active form. There is an equivalent neutral form for each function.

#(rs) "read string". This needs only one argument, namely the characters rs (remember the convention indicated above). The effect is to read a character string from the keyboard and the result is that same string. Since all characters including page and line control characters are permissible we need some special way to terminate input. TRAC uses a *meta character* for this purpose. In the basic system this is the apostrophe but there is another function which allows the user to change the meta character to any other character he chooses. The meta character itself is deleted.

#(rc) "read character". This is similar to rs excepting that only one character is read from the keyboard. No terminating meta character is therefore required so the meta character itself may be read by this function.

#(ps, X) "print string". The effect is to print out the

string represented here by X on the typewriter. The result is null. Note here that the actual string in the second parameter position is printed and not a form whose name is X. This appears at first sight to be very restrictive but we must remember that arguments themselves will frequently be the result of other function evaluation.

#(cm, X) "change meta". The effect is to change the meta character to the first character in the literal string X. The result is null.

#(ds, X, Y) "define string". The effect is to store a copy of the literal string Y in the form store under name X. The result is null. If a form already exists with the name X the old one is deleted and replaced by the new.

Thus the effect of the functions

#(ds, abc, The apple is red)

is to store the string "The apple is red" under the name "abc" and to return null value. In this particular case the function

##(ds, abc, The apple is red)

has exactly the same effect.

Before giving any more examples we must look carefully at the internal algorithm which governs the behaviour of TRAC. As we have indicated above there are two strings maintained internally, namely the active string and the neutral string. Associated with the active string there is a pointer known as the scanning pointer (sp) which indicates the next character to be scanned and associated with the neutral string there are two pointers, one of which is called the current location pointer (clp) and points to the next free space on the neutral string and the other is called the current function pointer (cfp) which points to the beginning of the parameter list of

the most recently encountered function. Since nesting of
functions is permitted the neutral string also contains back
pointers to the previous outer function (pfp) if one exists.
Note that since function evaluation takes place immediately on
completion of evaluation of the parameters only nested functions
can leave partially completed functions on the neutral string.
Fig. 3.2 illustrates the internal structure of the active and
neutral strings.

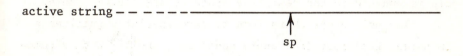

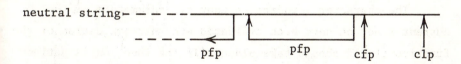

Fig. 3.2 Internal structure of active and neutral strings.

The algorithm now proceeds as follows. Characters on
the active string are inspected one by one and are usually
passed to the neutral string. The character # is never looked
at in isolation. Whenever # is recognised, the next one or
two characters are looked at to see if the combination is #(
or ##(. If neither of these combinations occur then # is
treated as a normal character. It also allows (in isolation to
have a special meaning, namely to commence a quote mode in which

all characters up to the matching) are passed from the active string to the neutral string without further processing. In doing this the outermost matching brackets are discarded. The recognition of #(or ##(has several side affects. Firstly these characters are discarded and a back pointer is put on the neutral chain indicating the start of the previous but as yet uncompleted function call. The value for this pointer is obtained from the cfp and the cfp has its value updated to the next available location on the neutral string. A marker is put on the neutral string at this point indicating the start of an active or neutral function as appropriate. Finally the sp is updated to point to the next character after (and the clp is updated to the next free space on the neutral chain.

The only other characters to have special significance in normal read mode (not quote mode) are, and). When a comma is encountered it indicates the end of an argument. It is deleted but a marker is placed on the neutral string to indicate that an argument ends here. The marker could be a pointer to assist in rapid chaining down the argument list.

The character) indicates that all parameters of the current function have been evaluated and that evaluation of the function itself should take place. If the function is active the result is inserted on the active string at the point indicated by the sp and the sp is set back to the beginning of the result. The clp is reset to the value of the cfp thus deleting all trace of this function and the cfp is set back to the start of the previous function. Scanning then continues.

If the function is neutral then the cfp is set back to the previous function, the result is inserted on the neutral string in place of the function which produced it and the clp is set to the next free space on the neutral string. Scanning then continues.

It should now be clear that the real difference between

56

active and neutral functions is that the result of an active
function is rescanned whereas the result of a neutral function
is not.

   We will now carefully analyse an example and will then
give a formal account of the algorithm which includes a little
extra "housekeeping" to the above informal description.

   We will suppose that the user has just been asked by the
system to type some information. A T at the beginning of a
line will indicate a terminal response whereas an A or an N
will indicate that the line represents the current value of
the active or neutral string respectively. We will indicate
the state of these chains as each control character is encountered using a comma on the neutral string to represent argument markers and # or ## to represent active and neutral function markers on the neutral string.

```
T     #(ps, #(rs))'              Comment note the meta symbol

A     #(ps, #(rs))...
      ↑
      sp

N     ............
      ↑            ↑
      cfp          clp

A     #(ps, #(rs))...
          ↑
          sp

N     ...., # ps ....            Comment the, has not yet been
      ⟵┘ ↑    ↑                                         passed.
          cfp   clp

A     #(ps, #(rs))...
           ↑
           sp

N     ...., # ps, ....
      ⟵┘ ↑      ↑
          cfp    clp
```

A   #(ps, #(rs))
                 ↑
                sp

N   .... # ps,# rs ....
       ⎣←⎯⎦ ⎣←⎯⎦ ↑   ↑
               cfp clp

A   #(ps, #(rs))
                 ↑
                sp

T   AUCHTERMUCHTY'   *Comment* Terminal response to read

                                request

A   #(ps, AUCHTERMUCHTY) *Comment*   Read function was
       ↑
       sp   active

N   .... # ps, ...
       ⎣←⎯⎦ ↑   ↑
        cfp   clp

A   #(ps, AUCHTERMUCHTY)
                       ↑
                      sp

N   .... # ps, AUCHTERMUCHTY ....
       ⎣←⎯⎦ ↑   ↑
        cfp   clp

A   #(ps, AUCHTERMUCHTY) ....
                       ↑
                      sp

T   AUCHTERMUCHTY   *Comment* system response

N   ....
      ↑   ↑
     cfp   clp

The effect then of typing in the line

#(ps, #(rs))'

was to cause the system to read input to the active string,

analyse it and print out the result. The final effect would have been the same in this particular case if the user had responded with

    ##(ps, #(rs))'

    ##(ps, ##(rs))'

or

    #(ps, ##(rs))'

since the second response involved no further processing. This however is unusual.

The function #(ps, #(rs)) is clearly useful to initiate the system. It is called the idling function and is automatically loaded whenever the active chain becomes empty.

3.3 *A formal description of the TRAC algorithm*

We give now a formal account of the TRAC algorithm which will follow very closely that given by Mooers (1966).

1.   Examine the character under sp, If there is no character left, that is the active string is empty, delete the neutral string, initialise its pointers, reload the idling function to the beginning of the active string, set sp to the first character in the idling function and repeat rule 1. Otherwise continue.

2.   If the character just examined is (then delete it and pass all characters up to but not including the matching) to the neutral string. Note that inner parentheses, function indicators and typewriter control characters are all passed without processing. Delete the matching character) update the sp and clp and repeat from rule 1. Otherwise continue.

3.   If the character is a sharp sign # followed by (
then the beginning of an active function is indicated. A back pointer is inserted in the neutral
string to the beginning of the previous function,
a marker is inserted to indicate the start of an
active function, the cfp is set to point at this
marker and the clp is set to the next free space
on the neutral chain. The sp is moved over the
two characters #(and the process is repeated from
rule 1. Otherwise continue.

4.   If the character is a sharp sign # followed by #(
then the beginning of a neutral function is indicated. The process is exactly as in rule 3 except
that a neutral function marker is set in the neutral string and the three characters ##(are skipped over by the sp in the active string. Otherwise continue.

5.   If the character is a comma then a marker is set
in the neutral string to indicate the end of an
argument, the sp and the clp are advanced and the
process is repeated from rule 1. Otherwise continue.

6.   If the character is a close parenthesis) then this
indicates the end of a function. The function is
evaluated and if it is active then the result is
inserted in the active string to replace the function call and the sp is set to point at the beginning of this result. The cfp is set to point to
the beginning of the previous function on the neutral string using the back pointer previously placed
there and the clp is set to point to the position on
the neutral string which previously held this back
pointer. If the function was neutral then the sp is
advanced one place, the cfp is set to point back to

the previous function on the neutral string, the
result is inserted on the neutral string in the
position previously occupied by the back pointer
which has just been used and the clp is set to
the next available position after the result. In
both cases the process is continued from rule 1.
Otherwise continue.

7.   The character is now known to have no special function. It is copied to the neutral chain, both
the sp and the clp are advanced one place and the
process is continued from rule 1. (If desired all
typewriter control characters which are not protected by quote brackets can be deleted at this
stage.)

3.4   *Some hints on implementing the TRAC algorithm*

The most efficient data structure for implementing the
active and neutral strings is almost certainly a linked list.
Since sub strings are frequently passed from one part of the
system to another, linked list techniques reduce the amount of
data movement to be carried out. The system needs only a forward linking since sufficient information is carried to handle
any backward movements which are required. It is also more
efficient when handling function evaluation if the parameter
markers are chained. Since the forward link is not known when
a new argument starts, another pointer must be kept to the start
of the previous argument so that the link can be filled in
later. This pointer must be stored along with the previous
function pointer when a new function begins.

No mention has been made of garbage collection excepting
when the idling function is loaded. In fact garbage collection
is very simple since the only cells to be returned to the free
list are those on the active string which have been scanned and
not passed to the neutral string and also the function parameters

on the neutral string of a function which has just been evaluated. It is simplest to make this garbage collection dynamic
rather than to call in a garbage collector when space runs out.

3.5   *Some TRAC examples*
       We give a few trivial examples to familiarise the reader
with the effects of the above algorithm. None of the examples
here has any real use.
       Suppose on request from the idling function we type the
response

       #(ds, X, Truth sits upon the lips of dying men)
       #(ds, Y, (#(cl, X)))
       #(ps, (#(cl, Y)))'

This causes a string named X to be created with value
"Truth sits upon the lips of dying men". It also creates a
string Y with value "#(cl, X)". Note that this function is
not evaluated at this stage since it was protected by quote
brackets. The final print statement produces the output

       #(cl,Y)

since it is also protected by quote brackets.
       If the final line were replaced by

       #(ps, ## (cl, Y))'

then the output would be

       #(cl, X)

since this time the call function is not protected by quote
brackets but is neutral and therefore copies the value of

62

string Y straight to the neutral string from where it is printed.

Finally if the last line were replaced by

#(ps, # (cl, Y))'

then the output would be

Truth sits upon the lips of dying men

since the first call function is active which means that the value of Y is rescanned thus producing the value of X. This is also rescanned since the value of Y was an active function but with no further result beyond copying into the neutral string.

The reader who doesn't follow these examples completely should trace through the action of the algorithm step by step using a diagram like fig. 3.2 as an aid. This is easiest done on a blackboard where irrelevant information can be easily erased.

3.6 *The remaining TRAC functions*

We will now carefully define a representative selection of TRAC functions and will then give a brief description of the remaining functions. Full definitions of them can be found in Mooers (1966).

#(ss, N, X1, X2,...). The effect of this function is to take the form with name N from the form store and to scan it looking first for any occurrences of the literal substring X1. Any occurrences of X1 are deleted and replaced by an internal marker which we will denote by *1. The process is then repeated on the marked version looking for remaining occurrences of the literal substring X2 all of which are replaced by an internal marker *2 and so on. The marked or segmented form replaces the old form in the form store under name N. The

result of this function is null. The substrings of characters
between markers are called segments and it can be seen that we
have created a macro body with formal parameters *1, *2,...
A null substring for one of the arguments X1, X2,... causes no
action to be taken apart from incrementing the marker count.

Thus the pair of instructions

    #(ds, song, ten green bottles)
    #(ss, song, ten)

eventually sets up the string

    *1 green bottles

with name "song" in the form store. Note that the pair of
instructions

    #(ds, gourmet, ten tender tentacles)
    #(ss, gourmet, ten)

would produce

    *1 *1der *1tacles

in the form store.

A side effect of the ss instruction is to set up a *form
pointer* which points at this moment to a position immediately
before the first character (or possibly marker) in the form
itself.

#(cl, N, A1, A2,...) "call". The *value* of this function
is obtained by fetching a copy of form N from the form store
and filling in the segment gaps *1, *2,... with the corresponding sub strings A1, A2,... If there are too few arguments
extra null strings are supplied. If there are too many then

the surplus ones are ignored. Note however that the evaluation of additional arguments can be used to produce side effects. The original form is left unchanged in the form store.

The call

    #(cl, song, five)

would produce the value

    five green bottles

whereas the call

    #(cl, song)

would produce

    green bottles

#(dd, N1, N2,...) "delete definition". This removes the forms N1, N2,... from the form store together with their names. If any of the names are not present in the form store list they are just ignored. The result is null.

#(da) "delete all". This deletes all forms and their names from the form store. The result is null.

The arithmetic functions in TRAC all perform decimal arithmetic using the decimal characters to the right hand side of the string specified and ignoring initial zeros. Thus if a string specified as an argument on which arithmetic is to be carried out has value

    X41P0103

it is the value 103 which is used for the decimal arithmetic.

The result of integer arithmetic is prefixed by the "head" of the first arithmetic argument. In the case above, the head would be X41P. Negative values are indicated by a minus sign. For all simple arithmetic overflow values are preset as part of the system. The final argument in any arithmetic function is always a default string which is returned as value in case of overflow. This default value is *always* regarded as having come from an active function and is therefore scanned. This enables appropriate action to be taken in case of overflow.

#(ad, D1, D2, Z) "add". The result is the sum of the strings D1, D2 as described above unless overflow occurs in which case the result is Z.

Similarly for the functions

#(su, D1, D2, Z) "subtract"
#(ml, D1, D2, Z) "multiply"
#(dv, D1, D2, Z) "divide"

There are two decision functions in TRAC and these are well structured.

(eq, X1, X2, X3, X4) "equals". This tests, character by character, for string equality. If string X1 is identical with X2 then the result is X3 and otherwise it is X4. This function looks rather weak until we remember that either or both results can be generated by function calls in the course of argument evaluation.

(gr, D1, D2, X3, X4) "greater than". This is a test of numerical magnitude on the string of decimal digits at the tail of D1 and D2 both being regarded as integers. If the integer D1 is algebraically greater than the integer D2 then the result is X3. Otherwise it is X4.

These are all the functions that we will require in our remaining examples so we will only briefly describe the others. As mentioned above full descriptions can be found in Mooers (196

Corresponding to the arithmetic functions there is a set of boolean functions bu, bi, bc, bs and br which perform the operations of boolean union, intersection, complement, shift and rotate. Rules are defined to ensure an answer in every case so there are no default options in this case.

A further set of functions handles the manipulation of characters and of segments in segmented forms. These are particularly useful in string handling problems. In each case the form pointer is used to indicate the next segment or character.

cs	"call segment"	returns next segment as value with default option if no segments are left.
cc	"call characters"	returns next characters as value with default option if no characters are left.
cn	"call n characters"	returns next or previous n characters depending on the sign of n as value. Again a default option is available.
in	"initial"	the mnemonic here is not good. This is used to search a string for the next occurrence of a substring. If a match is found the form pointer is left pointing to the next character. If there is no match a default value is returned.
cr	"call return"	resets the form pointer to the beginning of the form. Returns null value.

There is also a set of external management functions which are concerned with saving and restoring collections of forms which have been set up in a terminal session and are required for further use in another session. All these functions have null value.

sb	"store block"	puts into backing store a set of named forms under a common block name.
fb	"fetch block"	returns a named block of forms to the form store.
eb	"erase block"	deletes a named block of forms from backing store.

The final set of functions are the diagnostic functions. Although we mention them last they are very important and should be implemented very early on since they are invaluable in debugging the system as well as user programs. Again, all the functions except ln have null value.

tn	"trace on"	from here on the system types out from the neutral string the set of parameters of a function just before function evaluation. A backspace character allows evaluation to proceed. Anything else terminates evaluation and calls the idling function.
tf	"trace off"	terminates trace mode without initialisation.
ln	"list names"	returns as value the list of names of the form in form st

pf	"print form"	prints the body of named form together with segment markers.

3.7 *Some further TRAC examples*

The TRAC language is not immediately readable to the average layman (this is probably the greatest understatement in this book). Since the system was designed for the inter-active terminal and was intended to be general purpose one of its uses could be in interrogation systems or in computer aided instruction. The user of such systems cannot be expected to learn to program in TRAC and although much of his part of the man-machine conversation will be analysed and acted on by the system itself it would from time to time be useful if some of his responses could, unknowingly to him, automatically call some TRAC form from form store. Thus if the user's response to some question is "flapdoodle" we would like the system to generate the function.

#(cl, flapdoodle)

This can be done very simply by prompting the user's response by a read string function embedded as a parameter in a call function

#(cl, # (rs))

Clearly parameters can be handled in a similar way with the prompting questions being included as part of the parameter. It should be remembered that the print string function, like any other, is deleted from the neutral string after execution and so does not remain as part of the parameter. The reader should convince himself that execution of the following program

```
#(ds, service, ##(ps,(
what drink would you like?
))##(rs), ##(ps,(
what would you like with it?
))##(rs) #(ps,(
Your drink will be served at the Computer Centre Bar)))
```

with corresponding terminal dialogue

```
What drink would you like?
Whisky'
What would you like with it?
     '
```

could result in a neat whisky being served at the Computer
Centre Bar. Clearly the meta character used here is not very
suitable and could be changed to "." or to the new line character or something else.

If a program perhaps concerned with drill type exercise
is required to be repeated on termination of each call of it
then this can be done by making use of the recursive properties of TRAC functions. For example if a form with name
'Barman' in turn calls the 'service' form then the following
program

```
#(ds, dododo, (#(ps,
#(cl, #(rs))(
 ))#(cl, dododo)))
```

with initial response by each user

```
Barman'
```

will satisfy the liquid requirements of the whole university.

It would appear however that once started this process could never stop. This can be overcome, if desired, by having another form 'time gentlemen please' defined as follows

```
#(ds, time gentlemen please,(# (dd, dododo)))
```

which would remove dododo from the form store thus producing a null response next time.

A useful point to note here is that in TRAC a form may have null name. If the form list is scanned for a name which is not present it returns a null value. This fact can be used to initiate an error recovery routine if a wrong response is given by a terminal user.

To conclude these TRAC examples we give a complete program to solve the widely known problem of the towers of Hanoi. The solution given here is based on a solution by Professor van der Poel of Delft University.

The problem of the towers of Hanoi can be defined as follows.

Three pegs exist and on one of them are placed n disks in descending order of size with the largest at the bottom and the smallest at the top. The other two pegs are initially empty as shown in fig. 3.3 (see page 72). The problem is to move the disks to a similar final configuration with the disks being on a particular one of the other two pegs but only moving the disks one at a time between pegs and at no time placing a larger disk on top of a smaller one. This problem is less frequently but more accurately known as the problem of the Temple of Benares since a real situation exists there with an initial configuration of sixty-four disks of pure gold and three diamond needles "each a cubit high and as thick as the body of a bee placed there by God at the creation". Brahmin priests work unceasingly to transfer the disks according to the above rules and when the transfer is complete then "needles, tower, temple and Brahmins alike will crumble into dust, and with a thunder-clap the world will vanish". Fortunately even if the Brahmins make no mistakes, 18, 466, 744, 073, 709, 551, 615 transfers will be required at a minimum so we have little need to worry in the next few thousand years. I am indebted to Dr. C.P. Saksena for drawing my attention to this alternative deriva-tion of the problem. A mathematical statement and further information about the Temple of Benares can be found in Ball (1896).

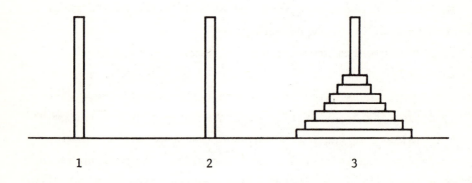

Fig. 3.3 An initial position for the towers of Hanoi problem

The solution to the problem is fairly straightforward if one thinks of it recursively. Rather than label the pegs 1, 2, 3 we will call them this, that and the other. The problem will then be to move the disks from this to that using the other where this, that and the other are any permutation of 1, 2 and 3. The recursive solution is then to move the top n-1 disks according to the rules from this to the other and

then to move the bottom largest disk from this to that. This
disk will now be in its correct position and will never be
moved again. Thus we only have to solve the problem of moving
n-1 disks from this to the other and our recursive solution is
apparent. The problem is of course trivial when n becomes
equal to 1.

One simple arithmetic fact that we will use is that if
a, b, c are any permutation of 1, 2, 3 then

$$a = 6 - (b+c)$$

We will start by defining a string called 'the other'

#(ds, the other, (##(su, 6,##(ad, this, that))))

and will then segment it on this and that

#(ss, the other, this, that).

This means that if we now call "the other" with parameters
having any two of 1, 2, 3 as values, the result returned will
be the other one.

We will now define a form called Hanoi with three segment
markers which will be marking the position of this, that and N
where this and that have the meanings above and N is the number
of disks to be moved.

```
#(ds, Hanoi, (#(gr, N, 1,
(#(cl, Hanoi, this, #(cl, the other, this, that),##(su, N, 1))
#(ps, from this to that)
#(cl,  Hanoi, #(cl, the other, this, that), there, #(su, N, 1))),
(#(ps, from this to that))
                         )))
#(ss, Hanoi, this, that, N)
```

The first line defines 'Hanoi' to consist of a 'greater than' function which tests if the value of N is greater than 1. If so then the next three lines are returned and these in turn, recursively move N-1 disks appropriately, "move" the bottom one and finally continue the solution with N-1 instead of N and "the other" instead of "this". If N=1 then only the fifth line is returned. Note the use of parentheses to prevent premature evaluation of function calls and also the final segment string call which makes this, that and N parameters of Hanoi.

The reader should convince himself that

#(cl, Hanoi, 1, 2, 3)

will produce

        from 1 to 2
        from 1 to 3
        from 2 to 3
        from 1 to 2
        from 3 to 1
        from 3 to 2
        from 1 to 2

3.8   *A brief description of GPM*

Since we have given a detailed account of the internal operation of TRAC we can now give a shorter account of GPM assuming that some of the concepts introduced above are understood. GPM is also a symbol stream processor and was originally written with system programming applications in mind. Strachey himself has said that GPM is now largely of historical interest but it is certainly interesting enough to include here.

The system takes a stream of characters as input and produce another stream of characters as output. Some characters are passed directly from input to output in copy mode but in general this process is interrupted by macro and parameter evaluation.

A macro call consists of a macro name, which always commences with the section sign §, followed by a comma and a list of actual parameters, each separated by a comma and with the last parameter terminated by a semicolon. For example

§F, A, B, C;

is a call of the macro F with parameters A, B, C. Unlike TRAC, although there are a few system defined macros in GPM, most are user defined and therefore F is not limited to a predefined set of values. Before the macro call is evaluated, its name and parameter are also evaluated and may therefore themselves contain macro calls.

In the macro body formal parameters are represented by the special symbols ~1, ~2,... with the convention that ~0 refers to the macro name itself. As usual the formal parameters are replaced by the actual parameters at macro call time. This contrasts with TRAC in which the formal parameters are marked internally by the segment string function.

The first system macro that we need is the one which allows us to define new macros. This is the macro DEF which takes two arguments, these being the macro name and the macro body.

Thus

§DEF, A, B;

defines a macro with name A and body B. GPM does not maintain a separate macro library but instead holds all information

including definitions on a single push down list. The definitions form a sub-chain known as the *environment chain*. In
this way it is possible to control the life time and scope of
a macro and for this reason, if a macro name is duplicated by
a new macro definition, the old one is not destroyed but merely pushed down to be restored when the life of the new macro
is terminated. The way in which this is done will become
clearer when we discuss the structure of the environment chain.
The philosophy behind this design decision is that DEF is just
another macro and since at the end of any macro call all trace
of the original call including its evaluated parameters is replaced by the result of the call then if DEF occurs within the
outer macro call, when the outer macro call is complete all
trace of DEF must be eliminated.

Angled brackets < and > are used as string quotes and as
usual on encountering < the symbol itself is discarded and all
following symbols including nested angled brackets are passed
to whatever stream is currently being used until the matching
> is reached and discarded. In particular all internal macro
calls are passed without evaluation. Macro bodies in DEF
macros are frequently enclosed in quote brackets to prevent
their evaluation at definition time. If this were not done
then whatever parameters were attached to the outer macro in
which the definition occurred would be substituted for the
formal parameters thus destroying them as formal parameters.

For example,

§DEF, A, <~1 is the ~2 of §~3, ~4; >;
§DEF, B, <~1 evil. >;
§A, love of money, root, B, all;

would produce

love of money is the root of all evil.

Note that the fourth parameter of the outer call is the first parameter of the inner call. Also the name of the inner macro call is not known at definition time for A.

GPM handles undefined macro names and insufficient parameter provision at macro expansion time in a different way to TRAC. In both cases in GPM an error exit occurs whereas in TRAC an undefined function name results in the null string being returned and insufficient parameter provision results in null parameters being supplied. The TRAC solution makes the system more flexible for the skilled user but creates debugging problems. These can be overcome by use of the trace facility at the expense of another run.

The whole of GPM processing can be thought of as symbol stream scanning but with source and destination streams varying depending on the current status or mode of the system. The input and output streams are the basic source and destination streams. When the symbol § is encountered the current output stream is temporarily suspended and output is diverted to an inner system stream. If § signals an inner macro call then the destination stream was already to this inner system stream so in this case the old accumulated information is pushed down to accommodate the new name and parameter evaluation.

The symbol ; indicating the end of parameter evaluation causes the corresponding macro body to become the new input stream but with actual parameters being supplied, without further evaluation, from the inner system stream. Both source and destination streams are thus being continually switched and information has to be stacked so that they can be restored correctly when the present operation is complete. The organisation of the inner system stream will be described in the next section.

Apart from DEF there are other basic or system macros available to the user. For example,

VAL, X;

returns the value of the macro with name X without any evaluation of this macro body. It is therefore equivalent to quot-
ing the macro body. It should be clearly understood that

DEF, X,<α> ;

defines X to be associated with the unevaluated string α and
then

§ X;

causes the string α to be evaluated whereas

§ VAL, X;

does not. § VAL, X; is therefore equivalent to

§ DEF, X,<< α >>;
§ X;

The basic macro UPDATE with two parameters A, B replaces
the macro body of macro with name A by the string B. At first
sight this may appear to be redundant since

§DEF, A, B;

would have the same immediate effect but globally, the effect
may be different since the scope of the new definition of A
may be different to that of the old. The UPDATE macro leaves
the scope of the updated macro unaltered. As implemented in
the original version of GPM UPDATE has an unfortunate restriction, this being that the new macro body must not be longer than

the old. This was simply a consequence of the way in which
macro bodies were held on the environment chain and is not
fundamental to the system.

There are also three system macros BIN, DEC and BAR
which perform decimal-binary conversion, binary-decimal conversion and binary arithmetic respectively. These can be used
to perform efficient arithmetic operations.

To complete this section we quote a few of the examples
given by Strachey (1965) and will leave a brief description
of the internal mechanism to the next section.

Suppose we wish to simulate in GPM the equivalent of a
conditional statement

$$if\ \alpha = \beta\ then\ \gamma\ else\ \delta;$$

which in TRAC we could do with the eq function

$$\#(eq,\ \alpha,\ \beta,\ (\gamma),\ (\delta)).$$

In GPM there is no system function to do this but the
following GPM macro has the same effect.

$$\S\quad \alpha\quad,\ \S DEF,\ \alpha,\ <\delta>;\ \S DEF,\ \beta,\ <\gamma>;;$$

If α and β are identical then the second DEF macro pushes
down the first and so γ is returned as the value of α when the
final semicolon is reached. Otherwise, the macro name β differs
from the name α and so δ is returned. This is an aesthetically
pleasing solution to the mathematician but is wasteful in execution time and is usually less readable than the TRAC eq function. That however, is a matter of opinion.

Another elegant example given by Strachey is for the
successor function SUC. Given an integer between 0 and 9 inclusive SUC will return the following integer. The definition

of SUC is

        §DEF, SUC, <§ 1, 2, 3, 4, 5, 6, 7, 8, 9, 10,
        §DEF, 1,<~> ~1;;>;

The macro body of SUC is a call of a function named "1"
which is defined in the course of parameter evaluation so that
its own macro body is ~n where n is the integer whose successor is required. Note that the symbol ~ survives evaluation
because it is enclosed in quotes which were not destroyed when
SUC was defined since they were inner quotes at that time.
The integer n comes from the parameter substitution at definition time for the macro "1". Thus when the call §1 is finally
evaluated its macro body simply returns the value of the nth
parameter which is therefore the value n + 1. (Remember that
2 is the first parameter of the call of §1.)

        The reader should now be able to convince himself that
with the definition

        §DEF, successor, < §~2, §DEF, ~2, ~1<<,> §SUC, >
            ~2<;>;,§DEF, 9, <§SUC, >~1<;<,> 0>;;> ;

a macro call

        §successor, 2, 5;

will produce

        2,6

as output whereas the call

        §successor, 6, 9;

will produce

    7,0

as output.

3.9   *The internal structure of GPM*

The implementation of GPM as described in Strachey's
paper is based upon the use of a stack with the basic item on
the stack being a character. Initially the source of the
characters being scanned is the input stream and this is indicated by setting a scanning state indicator C to zero.
Similarly a destination state indicator H is set to 0 initially indicating that the output stream is the destination
initially. The values of C and H may change as scanning proceeds but the old values must be saved so that they can be
restored when the current operation is complete.

A pointer S indicates the next free space on the top of
the stack. The characters < > § , ; and ~ are called warning characters and cause certain internal actions to take
place. If the character currently being scanned is not a
warning character then it is passed to the output stream if
H = 0 and to the top of the stack otherwise. In this case
the top of stack pointer S is incremented.

If the character < is encountered then a string quote
mode is entered and all characters including the warning
characters are copied to the destination stream indicated by
H until the matching > is met and the quote mode is terminated.
The enclosing < and > symbols are discarded in this process.
Since > should not be met in isolation it is used as an absolute exit to GPM if it is met outside the quote mode.

The character § indicates the start of a new macro call
but the macro call cannot be initiated until the matching ;
is reached. By this time the function name and all the para-

meters will have been evaluated and frequently this will involve calls to other macros. It is therefore necessary to include some pushdown mechanism so that pointers and source, destination states can be restored at the end of macro expansion time. This macro interruption may take place in two distinct situations. The first occurs while macro name and parameters are being evaluated. That is, before the corresponding ; has been encountered. Such interrupted macros are stored in a linked list or chain called the F chain. The other situation occurs when macro expansion is taking place and the process has to be interrupted because of a macro call from the macro body. Such interrupted macro expansions are stored on the P chain which is also a linked list. Both types of interrupts could have been stored in a single list but in this case further return information would have been required. Two additional pointers F and P point to the current entries on the F and P chains respectively.

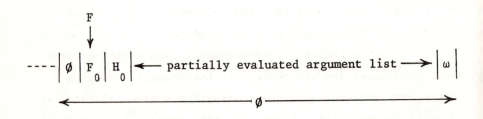

Fig. 3.4 A typical GPM F-chain entry.

A typical GPM F-chain entry is shown in fig. 3.4. The F pointer indicates the cell containing the address of the previous F-chain entry F_o along with the destination indicator value H_o for that entry. Note that it is not necessary to hold the source indicator since this will not have changed with the initiation of parameter evaluation. $\emptyset$ and ω which are really redundant but help in programming indicate the length and end of the current entry respectively.

Similarly a typical GPM P-chain entry is shown in fig. 3.5. In this case the previous source entry C_o is required

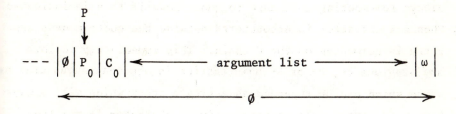

Fig. 3.5 A typical GPM P-chain entry.

since the current source will always be a macro body on the environment chain and the previous source may be another macro body or the input string.

The environment chain E is illustrated in fig. 3.6. The

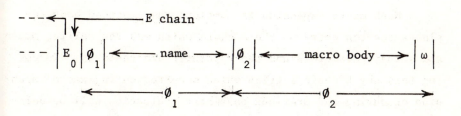

Fig. 3.6 A typical GPM E-chain entry.

entries here are the names and bodies of macros defined by the user where E_0 points to the previously defined macro and $\emptyset_1$, $\emptyset_2$, indicate the length of macro name and body respectively. For convenience the system macros are automatically loaded at the beginning of this chain. Since the E chain is scanned from the most recent entry backwards the convention for handling duplicate names is automatically realised. Note also that if a user defines a macro with a system macro name, his definition will take precedence.

The main scan now takes place as follows. Initially the source is the input stream and the destination is the output stream. Characters are passed from one stream to the other always remembering to change to quote mode if this is indicated. When a § character is encountered outside the quote mode a new entry is commenced on the F chain. This immediately follows any previous F-, P- or E-chain entries in one continuous area of store which can be regarded as a single stack which will always have a top entry. If another active § character is met then the previous F-chain entry is pushed down and so on until eventually the first matching ; is encountered. At this point the top F-chain entry is passed to the top of the P chain and the previous F pointer value is restored. Macro expansion now begins but may be broken off at any time if another active § is encountered. Parameter substitution which is indicated in the macro body by ~n for some integer n is direct from the associated parameter list. No further evaluation of the parameters takes place at this time.

When macro expansion is complete the expanded body replaces the top entry on the P chain which was the calling macro and actual parameters and the P pointer are restored. In doing this any E-chain entries which occurred during macro expansion or during the previous parameter evaluation will be deleted since they occur to the right of the F-chain entry on the stack. Finally control is restored to the next top F or P chain entry on the stack. It can be to either the F- or P-chain entry since either could have initiated the just completed macro call.

The only control character left to be discussed is the comma which is a separator for parameters. Clearly this involves placing either a marker or a pointer in the F chain to assist in picking up the parameters at macro expansion time.

A comparison of TRAC, GPM and ML/I will be made in the concluding section of this chapter.

3.10 *An introduction to ML/I*

The final part of this chapter is largely concerned with the general purpose macro generator ML/I which was designed and implemented by P.J. Brown. In this section we give a general user's view of ML/I and a brief description of its internal structure.

Like TRAC and GPM, ML/I is a string handling macro processor but unlike the other two it acts on "atoms" rather than individual characters. An atom is defined to be any single character other than a letter or digit or else any sequence of letters or digits bounded on either side by characters which are not letters or digits. To avoid having to repeat the words "characters which are not letters or digits" frequently Brown calls such characters *punctuation characters* and in non-mathematical or symbolic text this coincides with the actual meaning of this phrase. It should be remembered however that all characters such as +, -, § are considered as punctuation characters. In addition if page layout characters such as space, newline and tab are used these are also punctuation characters and hence atoms. Finally, to avoid any ambiguity a null punctuation character is assumed to precede and follow any complete piece of text thus ensuring that all opening and closing atoms are recognised.

We can illustrate here a basic difference between ML/I and TRAC (and incidentally with GPM too). In the Towers of

Hanoi problem discussed in section 3.7 we made use of a statement

FROM THIS TO THAT

and then segmented this string on the words THIS and THAT. We were careful here not to use the statement

FROM HERE TO THERE

with corresponding segmentation on HERE and THERE because TRAC would have recognised the four consecutive characters HERE in the word THERE and would have replaced them by an internal marker before looking for occurrences of THERE. It would then have not recognised the occurrence of the word THERE and the program would have apparently inexplicably failed, although the error could have been detected by use of the trace facility. The error would not have occurred if we had segmented in the order THERE, HERE but this would have been a bit artificial. The problem would not have occurred in ML/I since both HERE and THERE are atoms and their internal structure is never examined.

The simplest way of making a text replacement in ML/I is by means of a macro defined as

MCDEF P AS Q

where P and Q are both atoms and P is to be replaced by Q. Q is called the *replacement text*.

In this context MCDEF and AS are reserved words and a necessary part of the macro definition. The reserved use of AS is strictly local and the atom AS is not excluded from appearing elsewhere in the text. It can even be the value of either of the atoms P or Q.

Thus the macro

MCDEF PROF AS PROFESSOR

would replace every occurrence of the atom PROF by the atom
PROFESSOR.

Note that so far we have only replaced one atom by another
but it is possible and indeed usual to make more complex substitutions. The first extension is to allow multiple atoms for the
replacement text. This is handled by putting the replacement
text in quotes. For the moment we will use < and > as string
quotes but the user has to specify in a declarative statement
which characters he is going to use as string quotes. This is
essential in a general purpose macro processor since if the
quote characters are fixed they may appear in the input text
with some different meaning. Thus in some mathematical text <
may be in use with meaning "less than" and the user may pre-
fer to use § and $ as string quotes. This point will be dis-
cussed further shortly.

However, allowing for the present that < and > are string
quotes we can now write

MCDEF PROFESSOR AS
<THE HEAD OF THE DEPARTMENT OF COMPUTER SCIENCE>

and subsequent occurrences of the word PROFESSOR will be replaced by the corresponding string with the string quotes re-
moved. In particular an occurrence of the word PROF would be
temporarily replaced by PROFESSOR and then immediately by THE
HEAD OF THE DEPARTMENT OF COMPUTER SCIENCE. This is because of
the recursive nature of ML/I which rescans each replacement to
see if further replacement is necessary. This must be handled
with care since for example if we had made the definition

MCDEF PROFESSOR AS <PROFESSOR OF COMPUTER SCIENCE>

we would have entered an infinite loop continually replacing
the word PROFESSOR. This can be simply overcome by writing

MCDEF PROFESSOR AS <<PROFESSOR> OF COMPUTER SCIENCE>

In this case the outer quotes are stripped off at macro definition time and the inner quotes are stripped off when the
replacement text is rescanned. In this case the atom PROFESSOR
is not recognised as another macro name.

If several consecutive atoms are to be replaced this can
be done by the apparently rather clumsy device of writing for
example

MCDEF LITTLE WITHS MISS WITHS MUFFET
AS <OLD MOTHER HUBBARD>

with the effect that every occurrence of LITTLE MISS MUFFET
will be replaced by OLD MOTHER HUBBARD. The keyword WITHS is
used to indicate that a multiple atom sequence is to be replaced. In fact either WITH or WITHS can be used as keyword
here with slightly different meanings. WITHS implies that any
number of spaces (including none) can occur between the con-
stituent atoms whereas WITH means that no space may occur between the atoms. The use of WITH is not obvious at this
moment. The possibility of no space occurring between atoms
in the use of WITHS can however be illustrated as follows

MCDEF HEAD WITHS MASTER AS <MR. SMITH>

would replace both HEAD MASTER and HEADMASTER by MR. SMITH.
The macros defined above have been concerned with direct
textual replacement and have therefore not required parameters.
A general purpose macro processor would not be very powerful
if it did not include a provision for handling parameters and

ML/I does it as follows. If the name part of a macro is built up of more than one atom or multiple atom sequence then it is assumed that at macro call time actual parameters will appear in the gaps between these atoms or multiple atoms. Thus if the name part of a macro definition is

APPEND TO WITHS LIST.

then APPEND, TO LIST and the terminating character "." are single, multiple and single atoms respectively and at call time a sequence

APPEND X TO LIST Y.

would be recognised as a macro call with parameters X and Y. Note here that the character "." has the dual function of terminating the atom LIST and being an atom in its own right. We can also see the purpose of the keyword WITHS which forces TO LIST into a composite atom.

As usual the macro body must be able to make use of the call time parameters and this is done by using formal argument indicators

%A1., %A2., %A3.,....

to be replaced by the corresponding first, second, third and so on actual arguments at call time.

Thus a full declaration of the APPEND macro could be

```
MCDEF APPEND TO WITHS LIST.
AS < YPTR := YPTR + 1;
%A2.[YPTR] := %A1.;>
```

A subsequent call

     APPEND X + 1 TO LIST Y.

would produce the output

     YPTR := YPTR + 1;
     Y [YPTR] := X + 1;

A further extension is to permit options in place of the single or multiple atom delimiters in a macro name. This is done by using the code words OPT, OR and ALL as follows.

     HEAD WITHS OPT MASTER OR MISTRESS OR TEACHER ALL

would allow any of

     HEAD MASTER
     HEADMASTER
     HEAD MISTRESS
     HEADMISTRESS
     HEAD TEACHER
     HEADTEACHER

to be used as the macro name.

This facility is particularly useful in the analysis of arithmetic expressions where an option

     OPT + OR − OR x OR / ALL

would allow expressions using the four basic operations of arithmetic to be used.

In order that the macro body can be used to generate the correct code at expansion time it is necessary to have conditional commands. In ML/I these include an unconditional jump and a conditional execution. We will consider the conditional execution in some detail and will assume that the unconditional jump is similar. In addition to the system argument markers

%A1., %A2., %A3.,...

there are also system labels

%L1., %L2., %L3.,...

which can be used to label any line of macro body code (if the input is by cards we assume a new line for each card). Further the notation allows separate atoms or multiple atoms of the macro name to be referred to in order of appearance as

%D0., %D1., %D2., %D3.,...

Thus a test for a plus sign in the second part of a macro name could be handled by

MGGO L1 IF %D2. = +

The equality here is literal equality and this statement causes a branch to the line labelled %L1. if the appropriate atom is literally a plus sign.

A similar result holds for the statement

MCGO L1 UNLESS %D2. = +

L1 can naturally be replaced by Ln for any appropriate integer n but it can also be replaced by L followed by a simple integer expression which must evaluate to a suitable positive integer at expansion time. There are various conditions im-

posed on this simple integer expression which we will not en-
large on here.

The equals sign in the conditional part of the IF or UN-
LESS statement can be replaced by any of

    BC, EN, GE, GR

with meanings belongs to class, equals numerically, greater
than or equals or greater than respectively. If the general
IF statement is now written

    MCGO LEXPR IF ARGI COND ARG2

where COND is one of the above then the order of evaluation
is ARG1 followed by ARG2 followed by the application of the
conditional to produce a result TRUE or FALSE. If the result
is TRUE then the EXPR of LEXPR is evaluated and a branch is
made to the resulting label. Otherwise the LEXPR is not evaluated and sequential processing continues.

The general form of the unconditional branch instruction
is

    MCGO LEXPR

We can now write a conditional macro body as follows

    MCDEF SET = OPT + OR - ALL;
    AS <   L   3, %A2.
    MCGO L1 IF %D2. = +
                  S   3, %A3.
    MCGO L2
    %L1.   A   3, %A3.
    %L2   ST   3, %A1.
    >

The code generated will be 360 Assembler code as described in chapter 2. This macro will handle simple assignment
statements such as

SET P = Q + R;

producing

```
L   3,Q
A   3,R
ST  3,P
```

or with

SET PROFIT = CHARGE - COST;

producing

```
L   3, CHARGE
S   3, COST
ST  3, PROFIT
```

It would be easy to extend this example to handle simple
multiplication and division but to allow more than one operator on the right hand side we need some internal counting
mechanism so that successive operators and operands can be
picked up.

ML/I automatically provides three count variables T1,
T2, T3 to each macro call but it is possible to declare more
if required. These variables are strictly local to the call
and values assigned to them cannot be communicated directly
outside the macro call. There are also permanent global variables P1, P2,... which can be used to pass information between
calls.

The variables T1, T2 and T3 can be used rather like sub-scripts so that, for example, if T1 has current value 3 then

    %AT1.

is taken to mean

    %A3.

We can assign values to T1, T2 and T3 by using the MCSET statement. This assigns a simple arithmetic expression which must evaluate to an integer at macro expansion time to some macro variable. The following examples should have obvious meaning.

    MCSET   T1   =   2
    MCSET   T3   =   T1 + T2 - 1
    MCSET   T%A1. = %A1. + T1

where in the last case the value of %A1. must be a suitable positive integer.

The SET macro defined above can now be extended to handle variable length simple expressions. To avoid writing lengthy code and also the problem of operator precedence we will continue to restrict ourselves to the + and - operators. We will also assume that the statement ends with a semi-colon so a typical statement to be handled would be

    SET P = Q + R + S - T + V - W ;

but we must remember that we must also be able to handle something as simple as

    P = Q ;

A suitable macro body would therefore be

```
AS          L     3,    %A2.
MCSET       T1 = 2
%L1.   MCSET   T1 = T1 + 1
MCGO        L4 IF %DT1 - 1. = ;
MCGO        L2 IF %DT1 - 1. = +
MCGO        L3 IF %DT1 - 1. = -
```

Comment an error routine call and exit can be inserted here

```
%L2.        A  3, %AT1.
MCGO        L1
%L3         S  3, %AT1.
MCGO        L1
%L4         St 3, %A1.
```

With a macro call

```
    SET P = Q + R + S - T + V - W ;
```

this macro body would apparently produce the code

```
    L     3,Q
    A     3,R
    A     3,S
    S     3,T
    A     3,V
    S     3,W
    ST    3,P
```

There is however an important point concerned with the macro template that we have overlooked. The macro template using OPT as described above allowed the use of alternatives but did not specifically allow repetitions. In ML/I this is handled by the

95

introduction of a "nodal" facility to handle variable numbers
of arguments. In the macro template a *node* is indicated by Ni
for some integer i before the first alternative and repeating
Ni after each permissible alternative. Thus the SET template
could be written

    SET = N1 OPT + N1 OR - N1 OR ; ALL

The nodes N1 indicate that + or - signs can separate parameters
as often as required but since the character ";" is not followed by N1 it cannot be repeated and in fact is a terminator.

The example given above is simple but quite complicated
structures can be defined allowing branching to different options on recognition of a particular character or sequence of
characters.

There are a number of system macros and functions available in ML/I but we will only briefly describe these here.

Earlier in this section we mentioned that the actual
characters to be used to delimit quotes was a user decision.
It is necessary to declare these characters at the beginning
of an ML/I session and this is done with the use of the macro
MCSKIP. The simplest way to use MCSKIP is to type

    MCSKIP MT, < >

which defines < and > as quote brackets. Any other pair of
symbols could have been used but usually these are distinct
since the quote process involves stripping off the outer quote
symbols leaving inner matching pairs unchanged. Combinations
of characters may also be used utilising the WITHS option.
Thus

    MCSKIP MT, *WITHS ( ) WITHS *

defines the opening and closing quotes to be *(and)* respectively. The MT part of the MCSKIP macro are a pair of the possible options M, T, D which may occur here. The options have the following meanings.

M	matched option on.	The matching skip delimiter is looked for noting but not acting on inner matched delimiters.
T	text option on.	This means arguments of the text within quotes are copied over to the value text.
D	delimiter option on.	This means that the delimiters of the skip are copied over. Otherwise they are discarded.

The character % which in the above text was used to indicate the start of a formal parameter must also be declared with a system function

MCINS %

The character % can be replaced by any other atom or collection of atoms.

There are also a number of debugging aids and functions for string manipulation but we will not describe them here.

There is one very important way in which ML/I differs from both TRAC and GPM. This occurs during the macro expansion phase when parameters are being substituted in the macro body as output text is generated. In both TRAC and GPM no further evaluation of the parameters is carried out during substitution but in ML/I each parameter is re-evaluated each time it is substituted.

A simple example will illustrate the inherent danger here.

Suppose we define two macros

```
MCDEF HERE AS <THERE>
MCDEF THERE AS <HERE>
```

with the intention of interchanging the words HERE and THERE.
This will not work since on the occurrence of one of the words,
say HERE, an attempt will be made to substitute THERE which by
this time will have had its protecting quotes stripped off.
The scanning of THERE will cause a substitution of HERE and so
on ad infinitum. This can easily be overcome by use of double
quotes

```
MCDEF HERE AS <<THERE>>
MCDEF THERE AS <<HERE>>
```

thus inhibiting further parameter evaluation at substitution
time. The macro expansion time evaluation of parameters before
substitution enables expansion time modification of actual
parameters to take place but it has to be used with care as
illustrated by the above example.

There are many additional features of ML/I but we do not
have space to give details of them here. We will complete this
section with a brief description of the internal structure of
ML/I.

All storage of information and processing take place on
two stacks which are set up to grow towards each other in the
usual way to make maximum use of the free space available and
to avoid overflow until it is inevitable. The first of these
stacks FSTACK contains global information at its base including
global macro definitions and the permanent variables, some of
which have been described above. In addition the source text
is held on this stack together with some workspace for macro
evaluations.

The other stack, BSTACK, contains information which, by its nature is more temporary. For example corresponding to each macro call a block of information is set up on BSTACK giving relevant information to this call together with a pointer to the block in which it is embedded and other descriptive information relating to that block. At completion of the evaluation of this call the stack is reset to its state on entry. Local macro definitions are also placed on BSTACK since they are only operative temporarily and can be absorbed in the block structure being subject to deletion in the same way as enclosing macro calls.

Information about labels is also held on the BSTACK and its top is also used as very temporary working storage. Hash tables and hash chains are used extensively to speed up the retrieval of information and block headings are standardised for simplicity of use.

Fuller details of the way in which ML/I works have been given by Brown and Saunders (1971).

3.11 *The LOWL language and its use in implementing software*

ML/I is a stand alone macro processor and would be of rather limited interest if its design and implementation had been for one particular machine. It was however designed for transportability between different computers with differing architecture and configuration. The way in which this has been done is by using a specially designed simple language called LOWL to encode the logic of ML/I. Thus no matter how complex the logic of the implementation of ML/I becomes it is only necessary to map the statements of LOWL into the instruction set of the new host machine in order to bootstrap ML/I to this machine. This at least is the usual theory of bootstrapping but in practice it is rarely so simple. Technical problems such as fixed store boundaries can cause storage allocation problems and there are often parts of the implementation which

either cannot be described in LOWL or which would be too inefficient even if they can. Nevertheless a considerable reduction in the amount of coding required to transfer the software to a new system can be effected by the bootstrapping
technique and ML/I is no exception. Once an effective low
level language has been designed it can be used to implement
other software and this has been done in the case of LOWL. It
should be noted that once one version of ML/I exists this can
be used to convert the statements in LOWL regarded as macros
to the machine or assembler code of another machine. Many
other macro processors may also be used for this purpose since
LOWL is so simple.

The LOWL character set is restricted to the upper case
letters A-Z and the digits 0-9 together with the characters

$$, + - / * : ' [ ] ( ) = \$$$

and the page layout symbols of space, tab and newline. The
dollar sign is used in messages to signify a new line.

The statement format of LOWL is very simple. Each statement written on a new line consists of a mnemonic operation
code surrounded by tab characters and followed by a fixed number of arguments separated if necessary by commas. A null
argument is not permitted but often the letter X is used to
indicate that a particular argument is not applicable in a
certain case. Clearly such cases must be handled by the macro
body of the corresponding macro. Literals are enclosed in
quotes and optional labels enclosed in square brackets may precede any operation code.

LOWL has two data types, namely character and numerical.
An item of character data is a simple character in the above
set whereas an item of integer data is any positive or negative
or zero integer. This may result in some cases in different
size storage elements being used for characters and integers

but this is clearly host machine dependent. Numerical constants
are represented literally by the characters which compose them
but character constants are normally enclosed in quotes (the
exceptions need not concern us here).

There are three registers as follows

A   numerical register
B   index register
C   character register

The names of all variables, labels, constants and subroutines must start with a letter and be followed by a sequence
of not more than five letters or digits. All variables are of
type *integer* and are declared by either

DCL   name

or

EQU   name1, name2

where the first statement declares an integer variable and the
second gives an alternative name (name1) to a previously declared variable (name2).

There is also a set of LOWL statements for defining items
in tables and also a hashing technique for quick access to names.

Statements in LOWL look like simple assembler statements.
They have been chosen so that they can be converted by macros
into either single statements or simple collections of statements in real assembler languages for various machines. Thus
any logic of ML/I or any other software which can be written in
LOWL can be converted directly to the corresponding assembler
language. If the number of basic LOWL statements is kept small
then the task of writing the corresponding macros is correspon-

dingly small. On the other hand LOWL must be sufficiently powerful to allow straightforward coding of typical systems software.

We give a few examples to indicate the flavour of LOWL but
fuller details can be found in Brown (1971). We will describe a
few LOWL basic statements and show how they are built up into
stack and unstack operations. We will concentrate on numeric
operations but remark that similar character operations also exist.

The statement

     STI   FFPT, X

stores the content of the accumulator in the address *pointed at*
by FFPT without affecting FFPT itself. The character X is a
special case of a subsidiary variable which provides information
to the macro processor. With name X as shown it means that the
content of A does not need to be preserved in A. If a P were
used in place of X then it means that the content of A must be
preserved in A. For many machines this information will be redundant since the store operator will not affect the content of
the register whose value is being stored. X and P will always
have these meanings and we will not repeat them again.

     STV   FFPT , X

stores the contents of A directly in FFPT and

     LAV   FFPT , X

loads the accumulator A with the contents of FFPT whereas

     LAI   FFPT , X

loads A with the content of the location pointed at by FFPT.

102

```
CAV     FFPT
```

compares the content of A with the content of FFPT. This will
usually result in a condition code being set depending on the
result of the "comparison" being TRUE or FALSE but since different machines handle this in different ways the compare statement must always be followed by a conditional jump statement
and the two together will be combined to perform the appropriate action. In particular

```
GOGE    THERE
```

branches to the statement with label THERE is the result of the
preceding compare statement, regarded as a "greater than or
equals" comparison, was TRUE. Otherwise sequential processing
is continued.

```
AAL         N
```

adds the *literal* value N to the A accumulator and

```
SAL         N
```

subtracts the *literal* value N from the A accumulator. There
are of course other arithmetic and boolean operators but we
will not need these. In the applications given below we will
need to know how many basic units of storage (for example words,
bytes, etc) are used for each numeric variable. This is given
literally by a system function

```
OF(LNM)
```

which returns the number of storage units occupied by an item
of numerical data in the current implementation. We can there-

fore write

```
        AAL     OF(LNM)
```

to increment the A accumulator by this amount.

We need one other arithmetic statement which does not explicitly utilise the A accumulator. This is

```
        BUMP    LFPT , N
```

which increases the value of LFPT by the literal value of N. Clearly in some implementations this may incidentally destroy the content of the accumulator. To preserve uniformity it cannot be assumed that the content of A will not be destroyed.

We can now give a full example of stack operations using LOWL. We can define a parameterless macro FSTACK to stack the contents of A on the forwards stack (see end of section 3.10) as follows.

```
        STI     FFPT , X        Store A to stack
        LAV     FFPT , X        Load FFPT to A
        AAL     OF(LNM)         Add numeric basic length
        STV     FFPT , P        Store incremented pointer
        CAV     LFPT            Compare for overflow
        GOGE    ER              Go to error routine if
                                necessary.
```

A similar piece of code can be used for the backwards stack loading operation although here, for some design reason, the pointer LFPT points at the previous item on the stack and not at the next free space as in the FFPT case. The reader should be able to write code to do this BSTACK load operation first preserving A, then updating LFPT, restoring A and finally to stack the restored content of A. The BUMP operation can be used but remember that it may destroy the content of A.

It may appear that we have used the last few pages to describe yet another assembly language but this is not true. The purpose of LOWL is not only to provide an assembler-like language to enable systems software to be written fairly easily but at the same time to allow this language to be mapped unambiguously into the operations and data structures available on other real machines. The success of LOWL depends on how effectively this mapping can be done.

3.12 *Conclusion*

TRAC, GPM and ML/I are all string handling macro generators but TRAC and GPM use the character as the basic unit of information whereas ML/I uses the atom. This means that ML/I would not confuse HERE with part of the word THERE since THERE is an atom to ML/I. Although the design of ML/I was clearly influenced by experience of GPM it is nevertheless very different in practice. It has a very flexible format and its use of keywords makes it much more readable to the casual user. The facility to change the environment is also very important from the user's viewpoint. It is very frustrating to learn the intricacies of a macro processor only to discover that you cannot use it to process some existing text since a character which appears naturally in the text has some fixed and immutable meaning to the macroprocessor. TRAC allows the meta character ' to be changed but not the other control characters.

The method of formal parameter specification is different in each of the three cases. TRAC uses the segmenting technique whereby internal formal parameter markers are inserted in place of specified groups of characters. This is the most general method since the ~n of GPM and the delimiter techniques of ML/I can both be simulated in TRAC. It suffers from the disadvantage though that groups of characters which would be a proper part of an atom in ML/I may be unintentionally

marked as a parameter. With self written macros this presents
no great problem but when text is read to form a macro body it
can cause difficulties. TRAC has the added advantage that the
number of parameters at call time need not match the number of
segment markers, extra parameters being ignored after evaluation and null values being supplied when insufficient actual
parameters are given. The evaluation of additional parameters
at call time allows macro calls to have side effects. The extensive use of the null string in TRAC, including the possibility of a null name is particularly useful. In particular a
null named error routine can be used as an escape when various
error conditions arise.

The method of specifying repetitions of delimiters in
ML/I and the branching technique to groups of alternatives in
the macro template is a powerful facility. In particular it
allows complex algebraic and other constructions to be analysed by a single macro.

Parameter evaluation and substitution also differs in
the case of ML/I from the other two macro processors. Both
TRAC and GPM evaluate the parameters and then substitute them
directly without further evaluation. ML/I on the other hand
evaluates the parameters as they are scanned and then re-eval-
uates them each time they are substituted in the macro body.
This can again be a powerful facility but it also wasteful of
time when this re-scanning process is not required.

The concept in TRAC of active and neutral functions is
an interesting one. Apart from sophisticated use by the experienced programmer it gives the relatively unsophisticated
user a means of reducing the time spent in unnecessary scanning of results from previous evaluations.

We are unable to recommend a "best buy" from the three
macro generators described in this chapter. GPM is largely of
historic interest and is no longer in common use. TRAC has
the advantage of being a powerful macro processor embedded in

a time sharing environment and ML/I is truly a general purpose
macro processor which is easily transportable to new computer
systems.

3.13 *Bibliography*

The references here are largely to published papers rather
than to text books. The references to TRAC and to GPM are in
the main to the original papers by the designers of these systems. ML/I is rather different in that several references are
to private papers by P.J. Brown published by either the Cambridge or the Kent University Computing Laboratories. These
publications are available in most University Computing Laboratory Libraries. The book by Wegner contains descriptions of
both TRAC and GPM but these should be read rather critically.
Finally attention is drawn to a letter by Mooers in the A.C.M.
Proceedings (1968) in which the copyright status of TRAC is de-
fended. Before referring to your private implementation of
trac as TRAC remember to get official clearance - you have been
warned!

Ball, W.W.R. *Mathematical recreations and problems*; Macmillan, 1896.

Brown, P.J. The ML/I Macro Processor; pp. 168-23. *CACM*, vol.
10, 1967.

Brown, P.J. The use of ML/I in Implementing a Machine-Indepen-
dent Language in order to Bootstrap itself from Machine
to Machine. University Mathematical Laboratory, Cambridge, Tech. Memorandum 68/1, 1968.

Brown, P.J. Using a macro processor to aid software implementation; pp. 327-31. *Comp. J.* vol. 12, no. 4, 1968.

Brown, P.J. *ML/I User's Manual.* University of Kent, 1970.

Brown, P.J. *How ML/I works.* University of Kent, 1971.

Brown, P.J. *Implementing software using the LOWL language.*
University of Kent, 1971.

Brown, P.J. Levels of language for portable software; pp. 1059-
62. *Comm. A.C.M.* vol. 15, no. 12, 1972.

Mooers, C.N. & Deutsch, L.P. TRAC, A text handling language, pp. 229-46 Proc. *A.C.M.* 20th Nat'l Conference, 1965.

Mooers, C.N. TRAC, A procedure-describing language for the
reactive typewriter; pp. 215-19. *Comm. A.C.M.* vol. 9,
no. 3, 1966.

Mooers, C.N. Reply to letter "Language Protection by Trade-
mark ill advised" by B.A. Galler. *Comm. A.C.M.* vol. 11,
no. 3, 1968.

Strachey, C. A general purpose macrogenerator; pp. 225-41.
Comp. J. vol. 8, no. 3, 1965.

Wegner, P. *Programming languages, information structures and
machine organisation*; pp. 151-74. McGraw-Hill, 1968.

3.14 *Examples*

(1) Write a program in TRAC which, given an English sentence
terminated by a question mark, will return a word for
word German (or French) translation. Build up diction-
aries of words and their German (French) equivalent and
if a given word is not present in the dictionary make
your system request this information.

(2) Determine the output from the TRAC input:

```
#(ds, XYZ, (B## (cl,OH)NJ##(cl,OH)UR MX ENF#(cl, YOUSE)))
#(ss, XYZ, X)
#(ds, YOUSE, (#(rs)))
#(ds, OH, O)
#(cl, XYZ, ES)'
ANTS'
```

(3) Is the TRAC interpreter recursive? Give examples of how
the interpreter works in support of your argument for or
against.

(4) Write an interpreter for the TRAC algorithm implementing
the functions tn, tf, ds, ss, cl, rs and ps. Devise a
set of test inputs to fully test your implementation in-

cluding definitions of forms with null name.

(5) Write a GPM program to simulate the Fortran piece of program

```
        IF (X)     10, 11, 12
10      CALL SUB1
        GO TO 11
12      CALL SUB2
11      CONTINUE
```

(6) Devise a GPM program which given two single digit integers will form their sum. Your program can be as inefficient as you like!

(7) Write an ML/I program to replace all punctuation marks in a piece of text by spaces and to remove any of a given list of words from the text. For example the list may contain commonly used words such as A, AN, THE, AND etc.

(8) Rewrite the macro SET described in section 3.10 to produce assembler code for any machine you use.

(9) Criticise the LOWL language subset described in section 3.11 and modify it as you think fit to be useful to systems programmers. Compare your solution with the full LOWL language as described by Peter Brown and say why you think your solution is a better one than his. (If you don't think it is then you are not a computer scientist - this is a possible criticism of you and not of Peter Brown!)

4 · A mobile programming system

4.1 *Introduction*

About 1970 Poole and Waite published several papers on
the problem of transporting software between different computer
systems. Their main concern was the programming effort required to transport a major piece of software from one system
to another. The obvious solution to this problem is to write
the software in a high level language such as Algol or Fortran
and this is partially satisfactory in certain problem areas
such as scientific programming where such languages are fairly
satisfactory. Even in this case however there are still problems since both Fortran and Algol compilers are rarely sufficiently standardised to be able to accept all programs written
in them and developed and tested on some other machine. Even
if one restricts oneself to a basic subset of some high level
language, as soon as the problem to be solved becomes complicated one is either driven to writing low level language subprograms to improve the efficiency of the generated code or
else to use some of the host system facilities such as file
handling and both of these departures from high level language
programming make transportability more difficult.

The solution proposed by Poole and Waite is that of the
abstract machine model. The idea here is to design an abstract
machine which would be very suitable for running programs in
some problem area and designing the machine code of this abstract machine so that programming in that problem area could
be made quite simple. In terms of existing real machine languages the machine language of this abstract machine may be

quite high level in the sense that one abstract machine instruction may translate into a complex set of real machine instructions. The overriding consideration however in the design of such an abstract machine is the ease of programming in the corresponding problem area.

The abstract machine or soft machine (S-machine) as it is sometimes called may now be implemented by using a macro processor to expand each S-machine instruction into a set of instructions acceptable to the host machine. Sometimes this S-machine instruction translation will not be carried out in one step but rather in several steps passing through a hierarchy of simpler and simpler S-machines until the basic level is arrived at. Thus once a basic set of S-machines has been defined, implemented and debugged they can be used as a higher level basis for defining higher level machines in new problem areas.

With this approach one still has the problem of finding a suitable macro processor to use to realise the higher level S-machine in terms of the lower level ones. To ensure that a sufficiently powerful macro processor is available it is more satisfactory to design a special macro processor and to implement it on each host machine. There are two ways in which this is usually done. The first is by using the *half bootstrap* procedure as follows. Suppose that a version is written and working on some machine M and a version is required for a new machine N. It is assumed that an abstract machine description A of the macro processor is also available. It is then necessary to write macros for each of the machine instructions of A which will expand into the assembly language of N (or into some other language for which a compiler is available on N). The macro processor on M is then used to generate a version of the macro processor itself which will be acceptable to machine N. The problem with this approach is that the macro expansion is being carried out on one machine and the testing of the generated code is to be carried out on another machine. Provided all goes well there is no problem but in practice things do not usually go well and some debugging always has to be done and this is not easy when the two machines M and N are not physically near to each other.

A more satisfactory approach is by means of the *full bootstrap* procedure in which the difficulties of the half bootstrap approach are minimised by first implementing a "stripped down" macro processor on machine N and then using this to implement the more complex system on machine N itself. If this simple macro processor is written in some high level language which is available on most machines and care is taken not to use the more esoteric facilities of some dialects of such languages which may not be available on other machines, then this basic macro processor should be available for the full bootstrap with a minimum of effort. If no common high level language is available then either a new version of the basic macro processor can be written in some high level language on machine N or else a half bootstrap can be used to move it from machine M to N. Since the basic processor is so simple this should not prove too difficult.

Having got the basic processor working on machine N, all further bootstrapping can be done on this machine.

Poole and Waite now define an abstract machine FLUB whose machine language is suitable for systems programming and in particular for writing macro processors. This basic macro processor which they call SIMCMP is now used to expand macros corresponding to the machine instructions of FLUB and once these have been debugged they can be used to implement a more powerful macro processor called STAGE2. STAGE2 has been written in the FLUB language and so no further work is needed by the implementor. Once STAGE2 is operational it can be used to implement other soft machines, both those designed by the new user or others already in use at other centres.

The design of S-machines is not easy and a lot of research work is being done and requires to be done in this area. We will not discuss this problem here but refer the reader to a paper by Coleman, Poole and Waite (1974) and to a book by Waite (1974) for a discussion of some of the problems.

In the remaining sections of this chapter we will discuss the SIMCMP algorithms, the FLUB machine and the STAGE2 macro processor.

4.2 *The SIMCMP algorithm*

The first step in a full bootstrapping procedure is to design a simple algorithm which can be easily implemented in a high level language. The algorithm SIMCMP is really a very simple macro processor which can be implemented in some commonly available high level language. An algorithm by Orgass and Waite (1969) written in Fortran IV is published in their joint paper 'A base for a mobile programming system' and is also described in the book 'Implementing software for non-numeric applications' (Waite, 1974). We will not reproduce their algorithm here but will merely discuss the principles involved.

It must be emphasised that this is the first stage in the full bootstrap procedure and the algorithm is therefore very simple and unsophisticated. SIMCMP is a compiler in the sense that source language templates are translated by macro expansion into corresponding object code which may be assembly language or some higher level language.

The first thing that SIMCMP does is to read in four characters which will be used as flags, two in the templates and two in the corresponding macro bodies. The first of these is the source end of line flag which is the character which will be used to terminate a macro call. Each new piece of text is normally a macro call so it was not necessary to use special characters to flag both the beginning and end of a macro call. If a line of source text does not match any template then it is assumed to be in object code form and is output unchanged. It would have avoided unnecessary attempts to match such a line of output code if each macro call in source text had commenced with some other flag. It must be remembered however that SIMCMP is a very simple macro processor although it would not have been made much more complicated by a source text start of macro call flag. We will assume that at most only one macro call will appear on each line of source text and therefore any characters which appear after the source end of line flag can be regarded as comment. We will use the character 'full stop' (.) as source end of line flag.

The second character read is a parameter flag which is used to indicate the start of a formal parameter in a macro template. The macro template is of a fairly general form consisting of an arbitrary string of characters interspersed by parameters. Because of this generality the macro parameters need to be recognised within the template string and the parameter flag is used for this purpose. We will use the character @ as parameter flag. No further identifier is needed for a formal parameter since they are automatically numbered in sequence from left to right.

The third and fourth characters read are the macro definition end of line and the macro body parameter flags respectively. As mentioned above for macro calls, any character string following a macro definition end of line flag is regarded as comment. We will use the character semi-colon (;) as macro definition end of line flag.

The macro body parameter flag, for which we will use $, indicates that an actual parameter is to be substituted at this point. It is followed in the macro body by two characters, the first of which is an integer which indicates the number of the parameter which has to be substituted. Since only one character is reserved for this purpose it is implied that at most nine formal parameters can be used in a macro template.

The second additional character will take the value 0 or 1.
If it is 0 then the actual parameter *which is only permitted
to be one character in length* is copied literally at macro
expansion time. The characters copied are in whatever input
code is being used for the system. If the second additional
character has value 1 then the single character is converted
to a user defined internal code before being substituted at
expansion time. The only condition on this internal code is
that the internal representation of the digits 0-9 must be the
actual digits 0-9 respectively. A fifth digit read after the
flags gives the external value to be taken by 0.

The flow sequence in SIMCMP is as follows. Firstly all
the macro templates and corresponding bodies are read in and
structured into a list. This is necessary to allow the subsequent matching process to be carried out and clearly, if the
list structure is too crude, then the corresponding matching
process will be slow. The list of macro definitions is terminated by macro body end of line flags appearing in the first
two places of a new line of code.

After all the macro definitions have been read in the
expansion phase commences. A single source statement is read
starting from the first character of a new input line and terminating with the corresponding source language end of line
flag. A match of this source statement is now attempted against
the list of macro templates. The order of attempted matching is from the first macro template read onwards. The order
of macro definition is therefore important. The matching process is very simple since the characters must match exactly
excepting for the formal parameter flag which will always be
assumed to match the corresponding character in the macro call
and which will be stored away in an actual parameter list.
The only other characters which do not usually match precisely
are the source end of line flag and the macro definition end
of line flag which terminates both the template and lines of

the macro body. These however can be eliminated at the read phase.

If a mismatch occurs then the next template is tried and so on until no further templates remain. In this case the source line is regarded as literal text and is copied direct to the output stream. Otherwise, as soon as a match occurs, the code in the macro body can be sent direct to the output stream with the actual parameters being filled in as they are encountered. It should be remembered that there are two conversion types for parameters and that the same parameter may be handled in either of these ways in the same macro body.

For example the following macro definition

```
ADD TERM @@ TO SUM;
WRITE ('TERM NUMBER $10$20 HAS BEEN ADDED TO SUM');
SUM := SUM + TERM ($11$21);
```

with corresponding call

```
ADD TERM 73 TO SUM.
```

would produce the code

```
WRITE ('TERM NUMBER 73 HAS BEEN ADDED TO SUM')
SUM := SUM + TERM (73)
```

but the characters 73 in the first line would be in external code and the characters 73 in the second line would be in internal code. In this example there is little point in doing this since the second statement needs to be scanned again by a compiler or interpreter before execution, but if we had used machine code instead then this could have avoided further transformation of the code.

SIMCMP has one other property which enables it to gener-

ate a limited number of arbitrary unique symbols. Each macro
may have up to ten such unique symbols to call upon. They are
indicated by the macro definition parameter flag followed by
the character 0 followed by any of the characters 0 to 9. Thus
at macro expansion time when a macro body parameter flag is
encountered it does not necessarily mean that an actual parameter is to be substituted. If the following character is a
zero then a unique symbol depending only on the next following
character is generated. This unique symbol is in fact a three
digit number which has an obvious use as a label. It must
therefore be different for different calls of the same macro
and this is handled quite simply as follows. A variable in
SIMCMP is set initially to value 100 and this is used as a
base for the unique symbol generator. It remains at this value
for the whole of one macro generation phase and whenever a
symbol sequence $0n is encountered in the macro body the cor-
responding base is added to n to generate the unique symbol.
At the end of this particular macro generation the base value
is incremented by one more than the maximum value of n in $0n
encountered during the current generation. If no symbol $0n
has been encountered then the base is left unaltered. In this
way unique numeric symbols are generated for each new macro
call. The incrementation of the base value at the end of a
macro generation can be easily handled by setting a variable,
say MAX equal to -1 at the beginning of a macro expansion and
changing its value to n on encountering $0n whenever MAX < n.
At the end of this macro generation the value of the base has
simply to be incremented by MAX + 1.

An example of the use of the symbol generator is as follows. Suppose in some language we have a statement with macro
template

IF @ = @ THEN INCREMENT @ ELSE INCREMENT @;

and we wish to write our macro body in Fortran then we could
define our macro body to be

```
        IF ($10 . EQ . $20) GO TO $00;
        $40 = $40 + 1;
        GO TO $01;
 $00    $30 = $30 + 1;
 $01    CONTINUE;
```

and if the base counter had value 120 at the macro call

```
    IF (I = J) THEN INCREMENT K ELSE INCREMENT L.
```

then the code generated would be

```
        IF (I . EQ . J) GO TO 120
        L = L + 1
        GO TO 121
 120    K = K + 1
 121    CONTINUE
```

Note that the full stops in the .EQ. part of the macro
body are not recognised as source end of line flags since they
are declared at macro definition time.

The SIMCMP algorithm as described by Orgass and Waite
(1969) is rather difficult to follow since all the information
described in the above section is held in one linear array
LIST. Thus LIST(1)-LIST(4) hold the flags, LIST(5) holds
the internal representation of 0, LIST(6) holds the base for
the unique symbol generator and so on. In addition the macro
templates and bodies, the source text and the generated text
are also held in LIST. This makes it simple to call the SIMCMP
subroutine from a driver programme but more difficult to understand it.

We conclude this section by remarking once again that SIMCMP was deliberately defined as a simple macro processor for ease of implementation and consequent portability. It has no internal conditional structure and cannot therefore be used directly to generate optimised code. For the same reason, argument lists of variable length cannot be handled.

4.3   The FLUB machine

As we have already mentioned in section 4.1 the full bootstrapping principle depends upon the definition of a hierarchy of abstract machines each of which is designed for the solution of a class of problems. In order to bootstrap from SIMCMP to a more sophisticated macro processor known as STAGE2 we define an abstract machine known as FLUB (First Language Under Bootstrap) which has two fundamental properties. First it must be adequate as a programming language in which to write STAGE2 and second each FLUB machine instruction must have sufficiently simple format for it to be handled as a SIMCMP macro template with corresponding code generation. We will concentrate here on the definition of FLUB and leave the reader to verify that each FLUB machine instruction can be handled by SIMCMP.

The FLUB machine must provide data structures in which character strings, trees and integers can be handled and also a set of operations for manipulating the items in these structures. For this reason the FLUB machine is word organised with each word usually containing three fields.

    FLG   VAL   PTR

where

    1   FLG must be able to hold small integers as markers
    2   VAL must be capable of holding either characters or

integers specifying the number of characters in a
string.

3   PTR must be able to hold an address.

The size of the FLUB word and the fields within that word
are clearly dependent upon the real machine upon which FLUB is
to be implemented. In a particular FLUB word we could have for
example

     FLG = 0
     VAL = 100
     PTR = 1106

where the FLG value indicates that reference is being made to
a string of 100 characters starting at machine address 1106.

The FLUB machine also requires general purpose registers,
a processing unit, three I/O streams and a main store. To
avoid decoding problems, the number of registers is restricted
to 36 with single character names A,B,C,...,Z,0,1,2,...,9. The
main store is of unspecified size and depends on the available
store in the host machine.

FLUB has 28 machine operations and 2 pseudo operations.
The full list of operations are described in detail in Waite
(1973) and in various other joint publications of Waite, Poole
and others. We will only describe a few instructions here
which are typical of the various classes into which they fall.

We have first a set of field instructions which refer
only to fields of registers. For example

     FLG A = 0.

or

     VAL B = PTR C.

with corresponding templates

        FLG @ = @;

and

        VAL @ = PTR @;

For the remaining instructions we will give only the templates. There are two instructions to load and store registers and these are

        GET @ = @;

and

        STO @ = @;

A set of six arithmetic instructions include

        VAL @ = @ + @;

and

        PTR @ = @ + @;

as typical examples.

There are also a set of eleven control instructions such as

        TO @@;
        TO @@ IF VAL @ = @;
        TO @@ IF PTR @ NE @;
        TO @@ BY @;

```
        RETURN BY @;
        STOP;
```

and four I/O instructions

```
        NEW INPUT LINE;
        VAL @ = INPUT;
        PRINT VAL @;
        PUNCH VAL @;
```

and two pseudo operations

```
        LOC @@;
        END PROGRAM;
```

The only one of these instructions which does not have
an immediately obvious meaning is perhaps the pseudo instruction

```
        LOC @@;
```

This is simply a label defining mechanism for internal looping.
    An interesting convention in the FLUB machine is the
initial status of the ten registers 0-9. It is assumed that
these are preset to initial values which not only make available to the programmer the integer constants 0-9 but also important information about the machine configuration including
the bottom and top address of available store and also the
number of address units per FLUB word. By "address unit" is
meant the smallest addressable collection of bits in the host
machine. In many machines this corresponds to a machine word
which will be sufficiently large to hold the corresponding
FLUB word and so will have value 1 but in a byte addressable
machine for example the value will be greater than 1. This is

clearly necessary for advancing the instruction counter in the
FLUB machine. A table of initial values for the fields of the
FLUB registers 0-9 is given in table 4.1

Register	FLG	VAL	PTR
0	0	0	0
1	1	1	1
2	2	2	2
3	3	3	3
4	0	4	0
5		5	10
6		6	
7		7	Number of units per FLUB word
8		8	Bottom address of available space
9		9	Top address of available space

Table 4.1 Initial values of FLUB registers

The three I/O operations transmit information between the
I/O device and the VAL field with characters being translated
to their internal form on input and back to external form on
output. Special characters are needed for carriage return and
other page layout commands. In a more sophisticated system it
would be desirable to introduce a more comprehensive I/O structure including buffer, files and so on. In the basic FLUB
machine however a very simple I/O facility will suffice.

The method of implementing FLUB is now straightforward

using the macro generator SIMCMP. Because SIMCMP is so primitive it may be that this implementation of FLUB is not very efficient but this is not important. The main use of the first FLUB machine will be to allow a program for the STAGE2 macro processor to be assembled and once this first version of STAGE2 is available it can be used itself as a macro generator to produce a new and improved version of the FLUB machine which can itself in turn be used to produce a new version of STAGE2.

It will not usually be possible to allocate an actual register for each of the FLUB general purpose registers. The FLUB machine should however be as efficient as possible and a lot of thought needs to be given to writing the FLUB machine code macros since every instruction in some higher level abstract machine will eventually be translated to FLUB instructions which in turn will be transformed into host machine instructions.

Waite has pointed out that although the operations of the FLUB machine are easy to describe and can be coded in a straight forward manner, nevertheless it is a well known axiom in compute programming that it is impossible to write even the simplest co correctly the first time. The macro definitions are the abstra machine analogue of the hardware of a real machine and need to tested in the same way as hardware is tested at the design stag A comprehensive hardware test program has been written by Bashkow, Friets and Kerson (1962) and this has been adopted by Henninger to test the FLUB machine. This paper has not been pub lished but it adopts the same principles as that of Bashkow et It firstly tests simple I/O of single characters and then uses the fixed data in registers 0-9 to check comparison operations. It next checks through the arithmetic operations again using th fixed data in registers 0-9 and similarly the GET and STO opera tions. Waite says that the use of the test program has success fully eliminated FLUB machine errors on several implementations before real applications have been made.

124

4.4   *The STAGE2 macro processor*

The STAGE2 macro processor is a generalisation of SIMCMP
into what has become a conventional general purpose macro processor. The macro template is an arbitrary character string
interspersed by source parameter flags and terminated by a
source end of line flag. As with SIMCMP these parameter flags
are specified by the user giving some flexibility to the system.

Apart from the generalised macro template structure,
STAGE2 offers far more power than SIMCMP by the use of nine
possible parameter conversion types and a variety of processor
functions which may form part of the macro body. We will discuss these in more detail shortly but will first look at the
method of template matching which has been designed to make the
macro recognition phase more efficient.

As usual the macro call is matched against a stored list
of templates by matching the substrings of the call against
fixed substrings in the corresponding templates and identifying the actual parameters as the intervening substrings of the
call, which may sometimes be null. On occasions this may lead
to ambiguity problems. For example, using flags as defined in
section 4.2 a macro template

      @ + @ ;

can be matched in two different ways against the call

      A + B + C

That is, the first parameter could be either A or A + B
with the second parameter being B + C or C respectively.

Also, if another macro template

      A + @ ;

had been defined it would not have been obvious which template
to choose. Many macro processors use the order of definition
to solve both of these problems but STAGE2 uses a special algorithm.

It is necessary first to define the *weight* of an element
as the length of the shortest substring of the input line which
could match that element. According to this definition, the
weight of a parameter flag is zero since it can match the null
string and the weight of any other element or string of characters is its length. As templates are defined they are now
formed into a tree structure with each element corresponding to
a branch and with the branches leaving a given node ordered
according to their weights with the lowest weight first.

The structure thus formed is a tree organised dictionary.
A discussion of a list structured organisation of such a dictionary is given in Waite (1973).

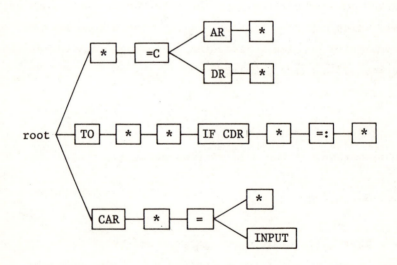

Fig. 4.1   Tree organised structure for some list processing
           templates.

Figure 4.1 shows a tree organised dictionary for the statements

```
* = CAR *
* = CDR *
TO ** IF CDR * =: *
CAR * = *
CAR * = INPUT
```

and figure 4.2 shows the modified structure when the statement

```
TO ** IF CAR * = CAR *
```

is added. There are a few points to note here. First an element already in the tree may have to be split when a new element is added. Thus in the above example IF CDR is split into two elements IF C and DR when the new template is added. In this example the parameter markers are denoted by * and for convenience at macro expansion time these have been made separate elements. Note also that spaces are important and must be left as part of the tree elements. Finally, ambiguity can

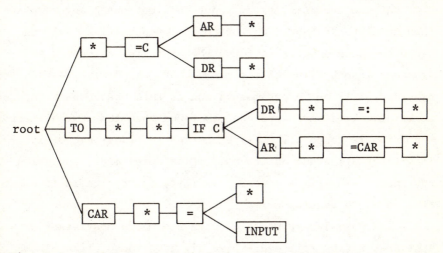

Fig. 4.2   Modified version of figure 4.1 when another template
          is added.

still remain as is in the top branch of figure 4.1 and here
the ambiguity is resolved by putting the branches in order of
definition.

The actual parameters used at macro expansion time are
normally character strings which may be null but it is essential that they must be balanced with respect to parentheses.
Thus with the example given above of a template

```
@ + @ ;
```

then any of

```
A + B .
(A + B) + C .
A + (B + C) .
```

would match this template with obvious actual parameters but

```
A + (B + C .
```

would not.

If the current line of input does not match any template
then the line is copied direct to the output stream. If on
the other hand a match is found the expansion commences and
proceeds line by line of the macro body. Each line is processed by filling in parameters and is then passed back for rescanning. If a new macro call is found then the current macro
expansion is temporarily suspended and the inner macro expansion takes place and on its completion outer macro expansion
continues. This is a powerful facility but can be inefficient
if deep macro nesting exists.

The formal parameters used in the macro body start with
a parameter flag followed by two digits. These, like SIMCMP
macro body parameters, specify respectively, the number of the

parameter in the macro template and the conversion type. Unlike SIMCMP there are nine conversion types. These are interesting and we give them in full.

0   the actual parameter is copied exactly.

1   the actual parameter is used to point at a memory address and the character string there is used as actual parameter. This is equivalent to indirect addressing. If the actual parameter does not point to a memory location then the null string is used as actual parameter.

2   as for 1, but with the difference that if the actual parameter does not point to a memory location then one is created and given the value of the symbol generator as contents. The symbol generator which behaves like that in SIMCMP is then incremented by 1.

3   The character immediately following the actual parameter in the macro call is used instead of the actual parameter. For the special case at the end of a line the null string is used.

4   Evaluates the actual parameter as an expression and returns the result.

5   Returns the number of characters in the actual parameter.

6   The line currently being constructed replaces the value of the actual parameter.

7   Initiates a repetition over the current line being constructed using "break characters" to split this line into segments. The break characters are those immediately following the occurrence of the formal parameter in the macro body.

8   Replaces the actual parameter by the internal representation of its own first character.

There are also a variety of processor functions which add further power to STAGE2. These include conditional assembly facilities enabling the processor to skip lines conditionally and unconditionally and also a looping command for a specified number of repetitions. Another function is used as a marker in this case to indicate the range of the iteration. Other functions allow direct copying of text under different conditions and also termination of either the current or all macro processing. Finally another function allows entries to be made in memory for use in conjunction with conversion types 1 and 2 above.

The implementation of the STAGE2 macro processor now takes place by using SIMCMP and the FLUB machine macros which can be handled by SIMCMP. A complex implementation program has been written by Poole and Waite in the FLUB language so provided macros have been written for FLUB on some host computer then STAGE2 can be bootstrapped on to this new machine. Since SIMCMP is a very unsophisticated macro processor it may be that a rather crude version of STAGE2 is obtained by this means. It can however be immediately improved by rewriting the FLUB macros for STAGE2 rather than SIMCMP making use of STAGE2's more powerful facilities and thereby producing a more efficient version of itself.

4.5   *Conclusion*

The STAGE2 macro processor has been designed so that it can be transported by a full bootstrap technique to different machines. It is then intended for use as a tool to implement abstract machines which are designed to make programming easy in certain problem areas. The main criticism of this technique is that it can be very inefficient both at macro expansion stage and at subsequent run time. The macro expansion inefficiency can be minimised by reducing the number of levels between the basic FLUB machine and the actual abstract machine

which is currently being used. Run time efficiency can only
be achieved by careful definition of the macros for each level
of abstract machine from the basic FLUB machine up to and including the machine of current interest.

The technique does however work and has been applied to
various problems including a list processing translator and
also a text editor. More recently Coleman, Poole and Waite
(1974) have reported on work being done in implementing a
Pascal compiler and also a BCPL compiler.

4.6 *Bibliography*

Bashkow, T.R., Friets, J. and Karson, A. A programming system
for detection and diagnosis of machine malfunctions;
p. 10. *I.E.E.E. Trans. on Electronic Computers*, vol.
EC-12, 1963.

Coleman, S.S., Poole, P.C. and Waite, W.M. The mobile programming system Janus; pp. 5-23. *Software - practice
and experience*, vol. 4, 5-23, 1974.

Orgass, R.J. and Waite, W.M. A base for a mobile programming
system; pp. 507-10. *Comm. A.C.M.* vol. 12, no. 9, 1969.

Waite, W.M. Building a mobile programming system; pp. 28-31.
Comp. J., vol. 13, no. 1. 1970.

Waite, W.M. *Implementing software for non-numeric applications*. Prentice-Hall, 1974.

4.7 *Examples*

(1) Implement the SIMCMP algorithm in some high level language. Even if this language is Fortran make your own
implementation.

(2) Design an abstract machine which can be used to implement a simple desk calculator. If you have STAGE2
available at your own installation implement this machine

and hence the desk calculator using STAGE2. Otherwise use your own version of SIMCMP to do this even though the result may not be very efficient.

(3) Prepare a tree organised dictionary list structure for the following templates

```
@ = @ ;
@ = @ + @ ;
@ = A ;
B = @ ;
@ = @ + @ + @ ;
I = 1 ;
```

Determine from your dictionary which template would be matched by

I = 1 + J + K .

5 · MP/3 – a top end macro processor with system facilities

5.1 *Introduction*

MP/3 was designed and implemented by S.H. Mandil (1973)
at the IBM (U.K.) Scientific Centre, Peterlee. At first sight
it appears to be just another macro processor of the ML/I or
STAGE2 type but with further study it is seen to have some interesting features which increase its power and flexibility.
In particular, like TRAC it has a degree of interaction in the
sense that it can prompt and accept responses from the user in
a time sharing environment. We will begin this chapter by
giving a brief description of the notation and basic facilities
of MP/3 together with some examples of its use. We will then
introduce the special features and discuss their relevance to
macro processing.

Mandil has applied his system to a number of large scale
practical problems and we will conclude this chapter by discussing some of these.

MP/3 has been designed for use both as a stand alone
macro processor and also as a processor to "sit on top" as it
were of another system and to interact with that system and the
user. For that reason it has been called a *top end* macro processor. This claim can be substantiated but in a limited way.
MP/3 has been written in PL/1 and the direct interaction with
another processor depends on that processor's ability to communicate with PL/1 routines. Clearly this is possible if the
host system is itself written in PL/1 or if it has a procedure
format which is compatible with PL/1 procedure format. This
naturally restricts the application area of MP/3 as a top end

processor but the idea is interesting and a study of the design criteria which allow this interaction is worthwhile.

5.2   *The basic notation and features of MP/3*

Within MP/3 there are four modes of operation, these being the *system, define, expansion* and *immediate* modes. The system mode is the top level of control to which MP/3 automatically returns upon termination of one of the other modes. In system mode MP/3 can accept and act on system commands and it can also recognise input which may initiate a switch to one of the other operational modes.

The define mode corresponds to macro definition mode and is usually entered from and always returns to the system mode on meeting the system commands $DEFINE (which may be abbreviated to $DEF) and $END respectively. Once in define mode the only possible exit is to system mode. This may be a temporary exit to system mode if a system command is met during macro definition.

Expansion mode which corresponds to a macro call can only be entered from system mode but a temporary exit to definition mode is allowed. Final exit is always to system mode.

In immediate mode an input line is compiled and executed immediately. The compiled code is not stored. Permissible changes of mode are shown in table 5.1.

Macro definition has the conventional format

```
$DEF   macro name
macro body
$END
```

where macro name is rather like that of ML/1 in that it consists of a character string interspersed by formal parameters, but since MP/3 acts on characters rather than atoms the formal parameters need to be explicit rather than implied. MP/3 is

		System	Define	Expansion	Immediate
	System	Yes	Yes	Yes	Yes
F R O M	Define	Yes	No	No	No
	Expansion	Yes	Yes	No	No
	Immediate	Yes	No	No	No

Table 5.1 Permissible changes of mode in MP/3.

unusual in that a macro name may begin and/or end with a formal parameter with a very special case of a macro name being a formal parameter only. The full formal definition of a macro name in extended B.N.F. where $\int_1^* \{X\}$ means "one or more repetitions of the character string represented here by X" is

<macro name> ::= <first part>|<first part><parameter>|

<first part> ::= <identifier>| $\int_1^*\{$<parameter><identifier>$\}$|
                <identifier> $\int_1^*\{$<parameter><identifier>$\}$

::= @ <inset> @

<inset> ::= <null>|()<null>|<separator>|()<separator>

<separator> ::= $\int_1^*\{$<character>$\}$

<identifier> ::= $\int_1^*\{$<character>$\}$

where <character> is any member of the legal character set for a particular implementation with a few exceptions. These excepted or special characters have a unique meaning to the system and cannot be used freely. This however is not so restrictive as it sounds since the particular characters used can be changed by system command to any other character which is not already in use as a system marker. We will not give the full list of default option special characters here but only those that we will use. They are

$$\$ \quad @ \quad \# \quad : \quad (\quad)$$

We stress that these are default options and can be easily changed by the ordinary user but from now on we will not keep on repeating this.

A few examples will illustrate the meaning of the different types of parameters. To avoid repetition of $DEF, macro body and $END we will simply write the macro names.

    DO SOMETHING

is an example of a parameterless macro name.

    PRINT @@

is an example of a macro name with a single parameter which represents any character string. The reader will doubtless wonder how this parameter is delimited at call time but this will become clear shortly.

    GIVE @,@ OR @@

illustrates a new idea. The comma between the first two @ signs is a separator and indicates that a list of actual parameters separated by commas will appear here at call time. The actual character or string of characters used as a separator is completely arbitrary with the exception of the special characters mentioned above.

        ADD @ () @ TO @ (),@

introduces two new ideas. The formal parameter @()@ implies
that the actual parameter used at call time must be balanced
with respect to opening and closing brackets. Thus an actual
parameter

        SIN (X)

is permissible whereas

        INVERSE)X(

or

        (OR [

is not. Similarly the second parameter @(),@ implies that each
member of the list separated by commas must be balanced with
respect to left and right brackets. If a comma appears before
the balance is complete the processor ignores this comma as a
separator and continues looking for a balance.
        To anticipate a little it should be obvious that a call

        ADD F(X) TO U, V(X,Y), W(Z)

is permissible. The result of such a call is still dependent
on the corresponding macro body which we have not yet discussed.
Note that the comma internal to V(X,Y) is ignored.
        The significance of blanks is left to the user. A rather
nice system facility called the "global squash length" (#GSQL)
squashes all strings of blanks in excess of the current integer
value of #GSQL. Thus if #GSQL = 1 then all strings of more than
one blank are reduced to a single blank and so on. If #GSQL = 0

then all blanks are eliminated and if #GSQL = -1 then all blanks are taken to be significant and left unchanged. The default option for #GSQL is 1.

We will now illustrate some of the facilities available in macro bodies. This will not be exhaustive but hopefully will illustrate the power of MP/3.

As a first example consider the following macro definition with three formal parameters.

```
$DEF ADD @@ TO @@ AND @@
 @2@ = @2@ + @1@;
 @3@ = @3@ + @1@;
$END
```

Note that although @@ is used to mark each occurrence of a formal parameter in the macro template it must be possible to uniquely identify each of these parameters in the macro body. This is done by using the notation @n@ for some integer n where n is the number counting from the left of the occurrence of the formal parameter in the macro template. Thus a macro call of

```
ADD 10 TO COST AND PETTY EXPENSES
```

will result in the output

```
COST = COST + 10;
PETTY EXPENSES = PETTY EXPENSES + 10;
```

As usual it is necessary to introduce macro time variables, labels, functions and statements so as to control the flow of code production at macro expansion time. MP/3 flags all macro time variables and labels thus avoiding the need for explicit declarative statements.

138

Local macro time variables start with the character #
followed by up to four characters from the alphanumeric set
A-Z, O-9 with the exception that the first character following
must not be G or F since these are used in conjunction with
to indicate macro time global variables and functions re-
spectively. In these cases #G or #F may still be followed by up
to 4 characters. Thus

       #X
       #GP12
       #FABCD

are examples of names of local variables, global variables and
macro time functions respectively. Local variables are strictly
local to the macro in which they are used whereas global variable values can be passed from one macro to another simply by
using the same name in both macros. MP/3 allows macro time
names of more than four characters but automatically truncates
them to the first four characters and issues a warning message
at the same time.

     A few macro time names are reserved for special system
use and the user should avoid them. These special names are

     TERM, CALL, IN, IND, INT, REM, TOPC and BOTC.

     It is a pity that such useful mnemonics should be re-
served and this is a minor criticism of the design philosophy
of MP/3.

     Since macro time variables are not explicitly declared
they do not have automatically set initial values. However
MP/3 issues warning messages if a macro time variable is referenced before it is assigned a value.

     Macro time labels are strictly local to the macro in
which they are used. They are flagged with the character $

and to avoid confusion with following characters they are terminated with the character :. Between $ and : there occurs the label name of not more than four alphanumeric characters. Thus

$LAB1:

is a label.

$REPEAT:

is also a label but its name is truncated to REPE.

One of the reserved names mentioned above was TERM which is the truncated form of TERMINAL.

#TERMINAL

is a system function which allows macro time communication with an interactive terminal. This is done by using #TERM in a macro time assignment statement. If #TERM is on the left hand side of an assignment statement then the value of the right hand side, converted to a character string if necessary is sent to the terminal. In any other context #TERM is a prompt to the terminal to provide input which replaces #TERM and is also copied to the system variable IN. There are other input/output facilities in MP/3 but we will not consider these here.

As hinted at in the previous paragraph macro time variables can be used in macro time statements including assignment statements. Such assignment statements are very simple. They are always flagged with the character $ on the left. No bracketing is allowed and processing takes place strictly from left to right. The values of macro time variables can be arithmetic, string or logical so a variety of operators for arithmetic, boolean algebra and string handling are available.

The reason for MP/3 evaluating from left to right with no operator precedence implied is now obvious. In order to give a meaning to each operator with permissible combinations of variable types, the left to right evaluation clearly indicates the order in which evaluation is to be carried out and a simple set of rules indicates which variables, if any, need a type conversion before the operator can be applied. If no such conversion is possible then an error message is printed. Thus

$\#T2 = \#T1 > \#T2 + 3$

is valid provided that #T1 and #T2 have values which can be compared by the greater than operator. If so then #T1 > #T2 yields the value 0 or 1 and so the final value assigned to #T2 is either 3 or 4. Otherwise an error message is returned.

Since only constants and macro time variables and functions can be used on the right hand side of a macro time assignment statement MP/3 allows the # sign to be dropped in this case. This can be confusing to the beginner and we will not make use of this convention.

Like other macro systems MP/3 also has macro time control statements. These are

$IF	with an implied $GOTO to the next line if the condition fails.
$GOTO	which is unconditional.
$EXIT	causes expansion of the current macro call to cease.
$QUIT	as for $EXIT but also stops attempting a macro match for any macro call in hand.
$FAIL	as for $EXIT but optional characters following $FAIL indicate alternatives for proceeding.

141

This is a very useful facility but requires a deeper understanding of MP/3 to fully understand. We will refer to it again later.

$PRESET   allows default values to be set for named macro time variables or formal parameters.

We give now a few simple examples which have been taken from the MP/3 user's manual and other publications of Mandil. The notation

    /* character string */

implies that the character string is to be generated as textual output.

```
$DEF MODE @@
$IF @1@ = O $#GMODE = O $EXIT
$IF @1@ = 1 $#GMODE = 1 $GOTO LAB1
$#GMODE = @1@ /* SYSTEM IN ABNORMAL MODE @1@ */ $EXIT
$LAB1: /* SYSTEM IN MODE 1 */
$END
```

The reader should now appreciate that this macro sets a global variable MODE to a value equal to the expansion time value of @1@ and if this is not zero then one of two messages is generated. Note that the three assignment statements to #GMODE could be reduced to one by making it the first statement to be obeyed.

Another example which illustrates the use of lists as parameters is the following. The lines have been numbered for ease of reference.

```
1.    $DEF INCREMENT @(),@ BY @@
2.    $#N = #FCOUNT (@1@) + 1 $#M = 1
3.    $L:
4.    #FELEM (@1@,M) = #FELEM (@1@,M) + @2@
5.    $#M = M + 1 $IF M < N $GO TO L
6.    $PRINT
7.    $END
```

Remember that in line 1 the first parameter of the macro template is a list whose elements are separated by commas and balanced with respect to brackets.

The second line contains a reference to a system function COUNT. This returns as value the number of elements in the actual parameter @1@ at call time. The effect of line 2 is therefore to set the local variable N to the number of elements in @1@ plus 1 and to set the local variable M to value 1.

Line 3 simply holds a macro label which could have equally been appended directly to line 4.

In line 4 the system function ELEM (@1@,M) returns the Mth element in the list which is the first argument in the corresponding macro call. This element will of course be a string of characters and it is this string of characters which is returned as value of ELEM.

Line 5 increments M and tests to see if macro expansion is complete. Line 6 is an output command which prints the generated code on the output terminal and line 7 is the usual macro terminator.

A macro call

INCREMENT X,Y(1,2),Z BY K

will now produce

X = X + K

```
        Y(1,2) = Y(1,2) + K
        Z = Z + K
```

Note that since the final parameter is balanced with respect
to brackets the comma internal to Y(1,2) is not treated as a
list element separator.

Another example to produce FORTRAN code from a special
PRINT statement is left to the reader to analyse.

```
     $DEF PRINT @,@ FORMAT @@ ON DEVICE @@
          WRITE (@3@, 50) @1@
     50   FORMAT (#FCOUNT(@1@)@2@)
     $END
```

The macro call

```
          PRINT X,Y,Z FORMAT F10.6 ON DEVICE 2
```

generates the object code

```
          WRITE (2, 50) X,Y,Z
     50   FORMAT (3F10.6)
```

Note that the COUNT value forms part of the code generated.

We have already mentioned a few of the system functions
in MP/3 but there are many more available to the user. For
example the LENGTH function returns the string length of the
corresponding parameter and the PICK function picks up a
specified substring of a given string. There are many other
such functions which the interested reader will find in the
MP/3 manual.

5.3   *The matching and expansion of macro calls*

As macros are defined they are added to a chain and macro

matching at call time is attempted in reverse order of definition. Thus if a macro has been redefined the most recent definition is that used.

After a successful macro match is completed the corresponding macro body is processed and some output is usually generated. This output goes to the output stack from which it can be printed as in a previous example or output in some other form.

Macro calls may be either *ordinary* or *flagged*. All the macros defined above have been assumed to be of the ordinary type and the text is continually scanned for such macro calls. The alternative is to specify a special macro call marker thus distinguishing a macro call from other input. This clearly reduces the overheads in scanning text looking for macro calls and is therefore useful when the text has been specially produced with this in mind. The global variable CALC is used to hold this special marker which signals the start of a macro call. By default the value of GCALC is null so initially the system is always in ordinary mode.

Nested macro calls are allowed but to avoid ambiguity all inner nested calls must be flagged at their beginning and end. The default markers for inner macro calls are (and) but we will use { and } to make some examples we are about to give more readable. It should be noted that if the system is operating in flagged mode then the mode flag must immediately precede both { and }. As usual, during processing of inner macro calls, outer macro calls are temporarily suspended to be resumed on completion of the inner call.

We will now consider some examples which illustrate some of the points discussed above.

Suppose we wish to replace a dot and cross product notation by a bracketed notation as follows:

$$a \times b = [a \ b]$$

$$a \times b \times c = \left[a\left[b \ c\right]\right]$$
$$a \ . \ b = (a \ b)$$
$$a \ . \ b \ . \ c = (a(b \ c))$$
$$a \ . \ b \times c = (a\left[b \ c\right])$$
$$a \times b \ . \ c = (\left[a \ b\right]c)$$

Here x has precedence over . and associativity otherwise is on the right. We are implying that an extended x product for example behaves as follows:

$$a \times b \times c \times d \times e = \left[a\left[b\left[c\left[d \ e\right]\right]\right]\right]$$

The following set of macros will effect this transformation

```
$DEF @@
@1@
$END
$DEF @@ x @@
[{@1@}{@2@}]
$END
$DEF @@ . @@
({@1@}{@2@})
$END
```

Note first that the order of definition is important. Scanning for macro matches takes place from the last definition backwards so dot products are recognised first but are not immediately expanded since inner macro calls delimited by { and } are evaluated first. Eventually these "dot" macros get down to "cross" macros which in turn get down to the simple quote macro. Thus the order of evaluation for

```
a . b x c
```

is that this is recognised as a call on the "dot" macro with parameters a and b x c. This macro outputs

(

followed by an inner call {a}. This only matches the first "quote" macro and produces

a

as output. The outer "dot" macro expansion is now resumed leading to a macro call

{b x c}

which eventually produces

$$\begin{bmatrix} b & c \end{bmatrix}$$

after a call on the "cross" macro and two inner calls on the "quote" macro. Finally control is returned to the outer "dot" macro call which terminates output with the character

)

Thus the complete output is

(a[b c])

as required. The reader should work through the other examples such as

    a x b . c
    a x b x c x d x e

and

```
a  x  b  .  c  x  d  x  e
```

The latter example should yield

$$([ab][c[de]\ ])$$

The above example was fairly easy since the associativity on the right was easily achieved because of the fact that input strings are scanned from left to right and therefore the innermost "cross" macro whose expansion was completed first corresponded to the rightmost cross.

The corresponding problem with associativity on the left appears at first sight to be rather more difficult. In this case the effect to be achieved is

$$a \times b = [a\ b]$$
$$a \times b \times c = [\ [ab]c]$$
$$a\ .\ b = (a\ b)$$
$$a\ .\ b\ .\ c = ((a\ b)c)$$
$$a\ .\ b \times c = (a[bc])$$
$$a \times b\ .\ c = ([ab]c)$$

and so on.

Because scanning is still taking place from left to right it would appear that the whole string has to be scanned before the appropriate number of brackets on the left can be output. This in turn suggests that macro time instructions must be used to count the number of crosses and dots and their relative positions. In fact this is not necessary since one can use the delaying properties of inner macro calls to achieve this effect. The reader who likes to solve puzzles should try this for himself before looking at the following solution.

```
$DEF @@
@1@
$END
$DEF @@ x @@
[{@1@}{@2@}]
$END
$DEF @@ x @@ x @@
{[[{@1@}{@2@}] x @3@}
$END
§DEF @@ . @@
({@1@}{@2@})
$END
§DEF @@ . @@ . @@
{({@1@}{@2@}) . @3@}
$END
```

Note that not all parameters in the macro bodies now initiate inner macro calls and also in the last macro for example a lot of inner expansion has to be completed before the outer macro is finally evaluated.

A macro call

    a x b x c x d

will be matched against the third last template with parameters a,b and c x d. The macro body will yield

    {[[{a}{b}] x c x d}

but nothing is output at this stage since the outermost curly brackets indicate an inner macro call. After {a} and {b} have been recognised as "quote" macro calls we have

    {[a b] x c x d}

which is recognised as another call on the third last macro
with parameters

[a b] c and d.

This yields

{[{[a b]} {c}] x d}

which in turn evaluates to

{[[a b]c] x d}

which is recognised as a call on the second macro yielding

[{[[a b]c]} {d}]

which after two more expansions of the "quote" macro produces

[[[a b]c]d]

as required.

This example illustrates that with a little thought
clumsy use of macro time counting facilities can often be
avoided yielding an elegant and efficient solution.

5.4   *Chains and structures of chains*

In many macro processors matching of templates is done
by a serial search of a single list of templates. This can be
very inefficient in terms of time taken to make the match and
becomes more and more inefficient as the list of templates
increases. Another disadvantage is that the longer the template list becomes the more difficult it is to ensure that the

150

order of the templates is correct for a given application. For
example in the last example in the previous section the order
of macro matching was essential to the solution. One solution
(Waite, 1970) is to establish a set of rules to resolve situations where a macro call matches more than one macro name but
this can be both complicated and time consuming. Another solution is to either provide macro definitions with limited scope
or else to allow macro definitions to be temporarily generated
during macro definition or expansion.

The method employed by MP/3 is to establish subsets of
macro definitions and to allow the user to specify which subsets are to be scanned for matching and in which order. Each
subset is called a chain and is given a user specified name
with the exception of the COMMON chain which is the subset to
which macros are attached by default if no additional user
command has been given. Thus in all the examples considered
so far the macros would have been attached to the COMMON chain.

An important concept is that chains may be joined or
broken dynamically thus allowing corrections to be made at will
in the macro environment. When an attempt is being made to
match a macro call the COMMON chain is always searched first.
The COMMON chain is said to be always active. For this reason
if full use is to be made of the chaining properties of MP/3
the COMMON chain should be restricted to a few basic macros
which may be needed at any time and which do not conflict with
other calls.

The system command

$CHAIN chain name

has the effect that all macro definitions which follow until
a new $CHAIN command is encountered will be added to the chain
with this chain name. If the chain name is new then a new
chain is created, otherwise any new definitions are merely

added to the existing chain with the same convention as before that most recently added macros are scanned first. As mentioned above the default option in the absence of a special $CHAIN command is the COMMON chain and one can always revert to the COMMON chain by use of the command

$CHAIN COMMON

The $CHAIN command merely creates chains and does not establish an active chain environment. This is done by the $JOIN system command with format

$JOIN chain1, chain2

The effect of this command is to "join" chain1 to the end of chain2 but without destroying the individual existence of either chain. The special case

$JOIN chain1

simply "joins" chain1 to the end of the COMMON chain. The real effect of the "join" is to cause the system to scan the chains for matching in the order in which they have been joined. Thus if we have the sequence of commands

$JOIN A,B
$JOIN C,A
$JOIN B

then the effect is that B has been joined to the COMMON chain, A joined to B and C joined to A so any subsequent macro calls scan the chains in the order

COMMON, B, A, C.

Chains may be subsequently disconnected by a $FREE command.

$FREE   chain name

"frees" *all* chains which have been previously joined to it. For example

$FREE B

will break the link between B and A which implicitly inhibits the indirect link from COMMON to A and C though B. It does not however break the link between A and C which may still exist for other purposes. Thus if

$FREE B

is followed by

$JOIN A

then a subsequent macro call will scan

COMMON, A, C

in that order.

Although one chain may be joined to several chains it is not permissible to join several chains to more than one particular chain. The reason is that a join of two or more other chains would lead to ambiguity during the search process for macro matching.

The system commands $JOIN and $FREE are global and as such may appear inside macro bodies if desired. Thus the fol-

lowing line is a permissible part of a macro body which is
executable at macro expansion time.

        $IF @2@ = 'ALGEBRA' $JOIN ALG $GO TO L1

        It should now be obvious that this facility both enables
the user to optimise the matching process and to modify the
environment according to the problem area.

        A useful debugging aid is the $MAP command which dis-
plays on the terminal a map of the current structure of chains.

        One final point concerning chains. Inner macro calls
may be associated with their own chain which may be different
to that associated with the outer call. For example

        {some inner macro call .A}

specifies A to be the environment for the duration of this call.
The system automatically reverts to the environment of the outer
call on completion of this inner call.

        In section 5.2 we mentioned the $FAIL system command and
we will refer to it briefly again here. In addition to $FAIL
we may also use

        $FAIL   (<parameter>)

where <parameter> may be either +, - or a chain name. The character + specifies that the current match should be abandoned and
the attempt to match continued at the next template on the
current chain. The effect of the character - is similar except
that the rematch goes up a level to the outer macro containing
the current one. Finally, if the parameter is a chain name then
the search is continued at the named chain of macro definitions.

5.5   *Integration of MP/3 with other systems*

As we indicated at the beginning of this chapter, MP/3 has been called a top end macro processor to indicate that it is possible to integrate it as it were on top of other systems. In this section we will review a few of the integration facilities available in MP/3.

First of all the reserved global variables in MP/3 can easily be made available to other systems which can therefore both take information from and give it to MP/3. The group of reserved variables can be regarded as a dictionary common to both MP/3 and the integrated system. This is most easily handled if the integrated system is written in PL/1 but is also possible with systems written in other languages. An example given by Mandil relates to the two system variables #GDIN and #GDOUT which stand for device in and device out respectively. In an interactive system it is possible for example to switch the output to the line printer if it is getting too large for the interactive terminal to handle.

Another communications area between MP/3 and its host system is the output stack. Two global system commands $EXECUTE and $LEXECUTE make the entire output stack or a local part of it respectively available to the host system. Both of these system commands automatically pass control to the host system which must eventually return control to MP/3. It is permissible for the host system to add information to the output stack thus opening another communication channel between these two systems.

Two external PL/1 variables help to access the part of the output stack made available to the host system by the $EXECUTE and $LEXECUTE commands. These are

OUT_STACK_PTR

which is set to point to the first byte of the data string in the output stack and

    OUT_STACK_LEN

which is a PL/1 BIN FIXED(15) variable set to the length of
the string.

5.6   *Some applications of MP/3*
        In this section we will discuss very briefly some app-
lications that have been made with MP/3.
        The first of these is an experimental urban management
system with two distinct user languages. The first of these
is English-like and the user is prompted for problem parameters
and the system responds with local government statistics. This
requires the establishment of a comprehensive data base containing relevant district statistics. Various macros are now
made available on the environment chain so that a user request
such as

    GIVE POPULATION, INDUSTRIES, PUBLIC PARKS OF PETERLEE

matches a macro template

    $DEF GIVE @,@ OF @@

and the corresponding macro body now produces code which can
be interpreted by a host system to produce the relevant statistics from the data base and return the appropriate output.
Unsophisticated users can easily be trained to type in syntactically correct requests particularly since macros are easily
written to remove redundant words and punctuation. An experi-
mental system of this type has been implemented and tested by
Mandil at Peterlee.
        The second language associated with this urban managemen

system is mathematically based and caters for the more mathematically experienced user. In this system more technically biassed statistical calculations can be initiated by the user using the same data base but a different environment chain of macros.

Mandil has also applied his system to symbolic differentiation and to the simplification of non-trivial algebraic expressions (Mandil, 1972) and together with Stamper (Mandil and Stamper, 1974) has designed and implemented a legally oriented interrogation language STAMPOL.

Finally a symbol manipulation language (Mandil and Pengelly, 1973) was used as an illustration in an educational television programme on symbol manipulation.

5.7   *Conclusion*

MP/3 is a fairly conventional general purpose macro processor but with comprehensive parameter types including lists with internal balancing of specified characters. It includes a large number of system defined and maintained global variables and also system functions. Only a few of them have been described in the preceding sections and there are a whole collection of debugging aids which have not been mentioned at all.

The most interesting feature of MP/3 is the environment chain concept which not only leads to an efficient macro matching process but also enables the user to resolve ambiguities in and necessary ordering of macro templates in a simple manner. Since the establishment of environment chains is dynamic it is possible for the system to switch from one environment to another depending on user responses. This would be particularly useful in an educational environment when, for example, computer aided instruction systems could be switched from one chain to another depending on the user responses. Thus both quick and slow learners could be accommodated by the same system even though the formal responses of the user were superficially identical. In this way, time consuming continuous testing for progress could be avoided.

MP/3 has also been designed as a top end processor with an interface accessible to other systems, principally those written in PL/1. Thus the power of MP/3 is made available to any system which observes the conventions of this interface.

5.8   *Bibliography*

Mandil, S.H. A macro processor as a generalised top-end to computing applications. *Software* 73, University of Loughborough, Leics. July 1973.

Mandil, S.H. *The MP/3 Macro Processor User's Manual.* IBM (U.K.) Scientific Centre, Peterlee, 1973.

Mandil, S.H. Symbolic differentiation and simplification using the MP/3 macro processor. Internal Report, IBM (U.K.) Scientific Centre, Peterlee, 1972.

Mandil, S.H. and Pengelly, R.M. A symbol manipulation language. Internal Report, Faculty of Mathematics, The Open University, Milton Keynes, Bucks., 1973.

Mandil, S.H. and Stamper, R.K. *The application of MP/3 to the design and implementation of LEGOL, a legally oriented language.* International Symposium on Programming, Institut de Programmation, Paris, France, 1974.

Waite, W.M. The mobile programming system Stage 2. pp. 415, *CACM*, 13, 1970.

5.9   *Examples*

(1)   Write MP/3 macros to convert a suitable subset of Basic statements to their Fortran equivalent. Explain how you would handle such concepts as the implicit availability of vectors of size 10 in Basic.

(2)   Write an MP/3 macro to convert a call

A = MATRIX MULTIPLY B,C,..., X, N

for a variable number of square matrices A,B,...,X of
order N to an equivalent piece of Fortran or Algol code
which multiplies the matrices B,C,...,X of order N and
stores the result in A.

(3)   Check that the macros defined in section 5.3 give the
right result when given the input

a x b . c x d . e

(4)   Rewrite the macros in section 5.3 so that the operator
"." has precedence over the operator "x" and check your
results with the examples given in section 5.3 and example 3 above.

6 · A boot strapped list processing system

6.1   *Introduction*

In previous chapters we have looked at several macro
processors most of which could be used as a means of generating
code for the language we are about to describe. During the
last decade many M.Sc. theses have been written on this topic
but the techniques are now so well established that the problem
is little more than an undergraduate group project in the application of macro processors to a well defined problem.

There is however an alternative approach which is worth
discussing and this discussion will form the basis of this
chapter. In brief we will consider a very simple list processing language with an unambiguous, almost trivial grammar and
will describe how a special purpose macro processor can be
written in a high level language to generate code by macro expansion. This is apparently an alternative method of achieving
portability since hopefully the high level language used will
be available on other computing systems. This is a well known
myth since local dialects and patois usually prohibit the immediate interchange of high level languages programs between
different systems but if care is taken by the programmer to use
only basic grammatical constructions and to use as simple in-
put/output conventions as possible then the transfer may not be
too traumatic. The obvious candidates for a high level language are Algol, Fortran and PL/1. Each has its disadvantages,
Algol principally in I/O and in basic Algol its string handling
capabilities, Fortran since it is principally an arithmetic
oriented language and has to be grotesquely twisted to handle

string processing and PL/1 because of its dependence principally on one manufacturer with widely different implementations
by other manufacturers where indeed such implementations exist.

In St. Andrews some years ago Fortran was the main high
level language freely available and for this reason an M.Sc.
student wrote a system in Fortran but more recently a small
group of undergraduates wrote a similar system in Algol W. The
latter system was far more elegant, not to say structured, but
naturally used the string handling facilities in Algol W extensively. In this chapter we will refer to Fortran code since
this is still more freely available than Algol W but hope that
the reader may be inspired to rewrite the system for a high
level language available on his local machine.

6.2   *WISP*

In 1964 Professor M.V. Wilkes published a paper entitled
"An experiment with a self-compiling compiler for a simple list-
processing language". The language in question was WISP and was
intended to be the nucleus of a list processing language which
could be extended by the use of subroutines if desired. The
system of compilation was very simple, the program consisting
of statements written on successive lines of the program and
each of which could be recognised by keywords which appeared in
the statement. The parameters were simple variables and appeared in fixed positions relative to the keywords. Thus a list of
standard forms which were simply macro templates with asterisks
indicating the position of the variables was scanned until a
match was obtained with the current statement and a piece of
code which was in effect the macro body was output after substitution of the appropriate parameters. The system was designed so that a compiler for WISP could be written in WISP and
the system could therefore be bootstrapped with the aid of some
initial hand coding of primitives.

Wilkes described a hierarchy of compilers each giving

more facilities than the previous one. We will only describe here the simple initial approach leaving the reader to investigate further if he so desires.

As in LISP (McCarthy, 1962) Wilkes divides the store into a linked list of cells each of which is divided into two sections known as CAR and CDR. Normally both CAR and CDR contain an address, but on occasions they may contain pure symbols Initially the CDR of each call points to the next cell in the list thus forming a single unidirectional list. (Readers who are unfamiliar with the concepts of lists and list processing should consult the book by Page and Wilson (1973) published in this series.) The letters A to Z are used for the names of lists which implies that a separate table of 26 pointers to cells of the linked list exists. Initially all of these pointers excepting for F are null and F points to the first cell of the linked list. By convention F is always used to point to the next available free cell. In a Fortran environment it is convenient to use a one dimensional array FREE to represent free space with adjacent odd and even cells holding corresponding CAR and CDR parts respectively. The list pointer will then point to CAR of its first cell.

The statement

P = F

with corresponding templates

* = *

means that a copy of the pointer in F is made in P so P points to the same list as F. It does not imply that a copy of the list F is made but simply that two names, P and F now exist for the same list.

Similarly

P = CDR Q

with associated template

* = CDR *

causes P to point at the second cell of list Q or in other
words P is the list formed from Q by dropping its first cell.
Again no separate list is formed for P and so a subsequent
change in P implies a change in Q and similarly a change in
the second cell onwards of Q implies a change in P.

Note that the statement

F = CDR F

is valid and causes the free cell pointer to advance one cell
down the list.

The statement format should now be obvious and so we will
only briefly describe the other statements required by Wilkes in
his compiler TRO.

The statement

CAR A = B

makes the CAR part of the first cell of list A point to list B
again leaving B unaltered.

CAR P = INPUT

makes a copy of the next non-blank symbol on the input tape into the CAR part of the first cell of list P and advances the
input tape one place past the next non blank character. The

pointer to list P is left unaltered. It should also be noted
that WISP is paper tape orientated and that if a version is
being written for a card input system then a tape input simulator must be written. A Fortran subroutine to do this could
be the following.

```
        SUBROUTINE INPT(CHAR)
        IMPLICIT INTEGER*2(A-Z)
        DATA NEXT /81/, BLANK /' '/
        DIMENSION CARD (80)
1       IF (NEXT.EQ.81) GO TO 2
3       IF (CARD(NEXT).NE.BLANK) GO TO 4
        NEXT = NEXT + 1
        GO TO 1
4       CHAR = CARD(NEXT)
        NEXT = NEXT + 1
        RETURN
2       READ(5,5) (CARD(I),I=1,80)
5       FORMAT (80A1)
        NEXT = 1
        GO TO 3
        END
```

This immediately shows the problems of the 'universally
available' language FORTRAN IV. Many readers will have to
guess that IMPLICIT INTEGER*2(A-Z) causes all variable names
starting with letters A to Z to correspond to half length integers and that the data statements sets initial values of
81 to NEXT and the value of the internal code for the blank
character to BLANK. They may even be familiar with the meaning
of these statements and not know that

        NEXT = NEXT + 1

will compile into inefficient code without the use of an opti-
mising compiler. However the important point here is that a
paper tape simulator can be written in FORTRAN for a card orientated machine and the FORTRAN code corresponding to

    CAR P = INPUT

would be

    CALL INPT(FREE(P))

where FREE is the one dimensional array defined above.

In order to allow branching within WISP statements
Wilkes introduces a numeric labelling. A label is a statement which corresponds to the null statement and has template

    **

That is the keyword is null and by convention the asterisks each represent a single decimal digit. Some labels, in
particular 77, have a special meaning which we will describe
later.

Branching statement templates are now of one of the
types

    TO **
    TO ** IF CAR * =: *
    TO ** IF CAR * = CAR *
    TO ** AND BACK

The first of these is an obvious unconditional branch.
The second branches if the content of the CAR of the first list
is identical with the final parameter. The use of : here implies that the following character is to be used literally.

The third is a straight branch on the comparison of the CAR
parts of the two parameters and the fourth is a subroutine
branch and implies the stacking of a return address. The
actual return after such a branch is implemented on reaching
a single statement

     RETURN

     There are also a few stack instructions required. These
include

     RESET STACK
     CAR * TO STACK
     CDR * TO STACK

with obvious meanings. The stack is used to hold parameters
and return addresses.

     With these few WISP instructions we can now describe the
working of the compiler TRO.

6.3   *A simple compiler for WISP*

     The compiler is in three parts. The first of these
reads in the macro templates or standard forms as Wilkes calls
them and stores them in the form of a list G with a full stop
indicating the end of the list. Each template in the list is
separated from the next by a comma. The WISP program to do
this is as follows

     X
     30
     G = F
     26
     CAR F = INPUT
     TO 25 IF CAR F =:.

```
F = CDR F
TO 26
```

The X at the beginning is a start symbol which triggers
off a routine to handle the initialisation including setting
up the linked list. If the compiler is to output Fortran code
then initialisation statements such as

```
IMPLICIT INTEGER * 2 (A-Z)
```

can be output at this stage. Readers who are familiar with
list processing languages should convince themselves at this
stage that this piece of WISP program does what it has been
said to do.

The next step is to set up a structured list D with
the CAR of each successive cell of D pointing to a different
macro template (see fig. 6.1). This list is used in the matching process and allows a quick transfer to the next template

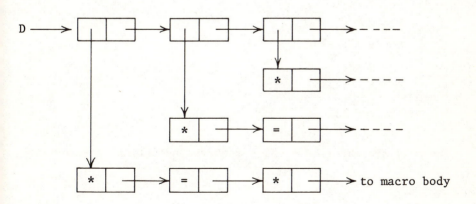

Fig. 6.1 A structured list D for holding macro templates

as soon as a mis-match occurs. In Wilkes' version each template is now terminated with a machine code address which is
a branch address to the corresponding machine code subroutine
which performs the appropriate internal action. In our case
the branch will be to the code generation phase of the macro
generator. The parameters as we will see have been placed in
order of recognition on the stack so are available for substitution in the macro body. The WISP statements to do this
are as follows

```
25
F = CDR F
D = F
23
TO 24 IF CAR G =:.
CAR F = G
F = CDR F
21
TO 22 IF CAR G = :,
G = CDR G
TO 21
22
E = CDR G
TO 79 AND BACK
G = E
TO 23
24
```

The only statement here which requires additional explanation
is

```
TO 79 AND BACK
```

This is a branch to a routine which plants the address of the corresponding machine code at the end of each template. As we have said above this will be a branch to the code generation phase in our macro generator.

A problem arises here if input is to be by card rather than by paper tape. Wilkes drops the comma at the end of each template but leaves in the carriage return control character at the end of each template. It is assumed that each program statement will be on a new line and the carriage return character is retained and takes part in the matching process. Card input can be made more efficient by separating each program statement by a comma and allowing more than one statement to a card. Our routine 79 will now have to plant a comma in the CAR of the list cell of each template rather than a carriage return as Wilkes does. We would appear to have to be careful to distinguish between the recognition of a comma as a literal rather than as a statement terminator but this is not so since a literal comma will be passed to the parameter stack automatically.

From now onwards we will terminate all WISP statements with a comma. To be consistent additional commas should be inserted on every line of all previous WISP program segments.

The final section of the compiler is the compiler proper which reads in the whole program, finds a match for each successive statement against the template list D and outputs the corresponding code. The program is terminated by two consecutive asterisks. It should be noted here that although the macro template parameters are marked with asterisks the actual WISP program will have actual parameters with names A to Z. The only exception is for literals where an asterisk or any other character can be used.

The input of the complete program to form a list P but with no attempt at recognition is carried out by the WISP segment

```
P = F,
29,
S = Q,
Q = F,
F = CDR F,
CAR Q = INPUT,
TO 28 IF CAR Q =: *,
TO 29,
28,
TO 27 IF CAR S =: *,
TO 29,
27,
```

The final step of the compilation section is the recognition of statements by template matching and the output of corresponding code. Remember that we have stored the templates in the list D and the program statements in the list P. Remember also that statements are terminated by a comma but that a comma may also be a literal.

The following program section to do this follows immediately after the label 27 above. A duplicate pointer to list D is made so that reinitialisation can be carried out for each new statement but the program pointer P is finally destroyed. Parameters are systematically placed on the stack and it is assumed that routine 77 picks them up for code generation.

```
E = D,
09,
RESET STACK,
Z = CAR E,
R = P,
05,
TO 13 IF CAR Z =: *,
TO 12 IF CAR R = CAR Z,
```

```
07,
E = CDR E,
TO 09,
12,
R = CDR R,
Z = CDR Z,
TO 14 IF CAR Z =:,,
TO 05,
13,
CAR R TO STACK,
TO 12,
14,
TO 10 IF CAR R =:,,
TO 07,
10,
CDR Z TO STACK,
TO 77 AND BACK,
P = CDR R,
TO 11 IF CAR P =: *,
TO 27,
11,
EXIT,
**
```

This completes the description of the WISP compiler which it must be immediately admitted is very crude. In fairness to Wilkes it should be emphasised that this was only the first of a series of compilers the others being more sophisticated and powerful. The simple compiler described here will be sufficient for our purpose and the reader is referred to Wilkes' paper for further information.

6.4   *Code generation for a Fortran version of the WISP compiler*
     Note that we have only to write a program which will read

in and translate the compiler itself. Subsequent translation of other programs will then be carried out by the compiled compiler. Additional statement templates can be added at this stage thus extending the language without modifying the WISP statements of the compiler. There are of course hidden penalties to be paid but these are relatively easy to handle. Firstly the initial template list, which is part of the data, must have these new templates added. Secondly the routine 79 which in Wilkes' version issues machine code labels must be modified. In our case this routine will be issuing macro identifiers and since these are for internal use only there is no reason why they should not be integers. We will therefore assume that routine 79 numbers the templates in the order in which they appear in the initial list and thus our routine 79 will need no modification to handle additional, or a reduced number, of templates.

Before looking at the compile routine itself we will consider Fortran code for the various WISP instructions. Many of the WISP instructions can be translated into single FORTRAN statements and this is the reason why it is more suited to macro generation rather than a succession of subroutine calls each with its overhead of calling code and parameter passing. We assume that a free list integer vector FREE has been set up considering each consecutive odd and even numbered pair of cells as the CAR and CDR parts of a single list cell. We also assume that initially each CDR cell contains the index of the next CAR cell. That is, the even numbered cells of FREE contain the numbers 3, 5, 7,... respectively. Furthermore, the simple integer variables A, B,..., Z are initially all zero with the exception of F which has initial value 1.

The equivalence of the following WISP and FORTRAN statements should now be obvious.

WISP STATEMENT	FORTRAN CODING
X,	CALL INIT
30,	30 CONTINUE
G = F	G = F
26,	26 CONTINUE
CAR F = INPUT,	CALL INPT (FREE(F))
TO 25 IF CAR F =:.,	IF(FREE(F).EQ.DOT)GO TO 25
	C "DOT" IS INITIALISED TO '.'
F = CDR F,	F = FREE (F+1)
TO 26,	GO TO 26

The routine INIT is assumed to set up the free space and
pointer list and also to output the header statements for the
program about to be compiled. These can be standardised for
all programs with the loss of a little efficiency and will
include a call to INIT itself.

Statements such as

F = CDR F,

have a single statement equivalent as shown above.

The use of the CONTINUE statement with a label is rather
crude but this can easily be cleared up within the compile
routine by holding back output of the label until the next
statement has been read. This would cause difficulties if a
programmer legally but irrelevantly writes two labels in
succession and uses them both for branching but this could
also easily be handled by the compile routine.

For the compiler the statement

TO 79 AND BACK

is very specialised. It has to place a comma in CAR G and a
macro number in CDR G. Since the macro number has to be in-

creased for each new template it is better to do this with a subroutine which increments a counter initially set to 1. Thus this statement will be replaced by

CALL SUB79

and SUB79 must be written to behave as above.

Similarly

TO 77 AND BACK

will be replaced by

CALL SUB77

and SUB77 will be the code generation routine yet to be described.

The stack operations require their own linear array STACK and a stack pointer PTR. For the moment we will forget about the problems of possible stack overflow and will just generate code immediately. For more sophisticated use it would be better to call a subroutine to handle the stack.

We therefore have the additional equivalent code

WISP STATEMENTS	FORTRAN CODING
RESET STACK,	PTR = 1
CAR A TO STACK,	STACK(PTR) = FREE(A)
	PTR = PTR + 1
CDR B TO STACK,	STACK(PTR) = FREE(B+1)
	PTR = PTR + 1

Equivalent code generation for the other statements is left as an exercise for the reader.

The compile routine which is our simple macrogenerator

is now almost trivial to write. As we have seen above the current macro number is stored in CDR G, that is in FREE(G+1) and the corresponding parameters are stored in order in the vector STACK. It is therefore only a question of outputting the appropriate code. There are two ways of doing this. The first is to branch by a COMPUTED GO TO statement to a WRITE statement whose corresponding FORMAT statement contains the necessary code. For example the statement

TO ** IF CAR * = CAR * ,

with say internal numbering 10 could cause a branch to FORTRAN label 100 in SUB77 where the following code would be planted.

```
100 WRITE(5,101) STACK(3), STACK(4), STACK(1), STACK(2)
101 FORMAT(7X, 'IF(FREE(',A1,').EQ.FREE(',A1,')) GO TO ',2A1)
    RETURN
```

This is probably the simplest way to write SUB77 but involves a recompilation of the subroutine each time a new WISP statement type is added.

A more flexible method is to store all the macro bodies in alphanumeric form in a vector with the parameter holes indicated by pointers from one to the next and with an associated array indicating the start point and first parameter of each macro body. This code is then moved to an output area where the parameters are filled in before final output. With this solution new statement types can be added without recompilation by an optional READ statement on first, or indeed any, entry to SUB77.

The final stage is to produce a starter routine which will carry out the very first compilation of the compiler. This can be done by handcoding from the WISP version to the Fortran version by direct substitution of the macro code for each WISP statement.

A more elegant method is to simulate the action of the compiler by calling SUB77 from a driver routine which simply reads in the macro number and parameter list for each WISP statement, plants them in CDR G, where G can be given any value, say 1, and in STACK respectively and then calls SUB77.

6.5 *Conclusion*

The purpose of this chapter has been to introduce a language which is ideally suited to macro generation methods and to trace through the implementation of a simple compiler for this language. The TRO compiler described here is the simplest and least interesting of Wilkes' compilers, full details of which are given in his paper. Included in this paper is a description of a WISP symbolic differentiation program which can be run once one of the more advanced compilers has been implemented For the enthusiastic detective it is noted that there are two errors in this program, one a typing error and the other a logical error. No prize is offered for their detection.

The WISP compiler described here can be generated using any of the macro processors described in earlier chapters. The justification for including it here is partly as an exercise in writing a specialised macro processor in a high level language, thus giving some degree of portability and partly to illustrate how a simple compiler of this type can be extended without re-compilation.

6.6 *Bibliography*

McCarthy, J. *et al. LISP 1.5 Programmer's Manual.* M.I.T. Press, 1962.

Page, E.S. and Wilson, L.B. *Information Representation and Manipulation in a Computer,* C.U.P., 1973.

Wilkes, M.V. An experiment with a self-compiling Compiler for a simple list-processing language; pp. 1-48. *Annual*

6.7 *Examples*

(1) Write equivalent code in any high level language for the WISP basic statements. Use the system outlined above for data representation or redesign it to suit your own system.

(2) Write the various subroutines outlined above in the same language.

(3) Implement the WISP TRO compiler and illustrate that it will compile itself.

(4) The WISP compiler as described above has no error detecting or recovery safeguards. Modify the compiler to detect errors and to print out statements which are in error. If you have access to a timesharing system, allow the user on-line correction of invalid statements with your compiler restarting correctly.

7 · Syntax macros

7.1 *Introduction*

All of the macro generators we have considered so far
have been of the text macro type. Although their individual
definition and implementation has been very different they
have almost all shared a common feature in that they could
have been implemented as preprocessors to the compiler for
the base language. The reason for this is that apart possibly from their own structure of macro calls the context in
which they are used is not dependent on the syntax of the
base language in which they are embedded. Thus in general
they could have been recognised and expanded by a preprocessor
at or before the lexical analysis stage with little or no
dependence on the embedding base language. TRAC is rather
different to the others since it is wholly interpretive and
textual evaluation may involve several levels of scanning with
possible user interaction at any level. It nevertheless shares
the common feature with the other macro processors that we have
described so far in that it is not embedded in some other system and even though its output may be destined for some other
system it is not itself influenced directly by that system.
Similarly, although MP/3 has been described as a top end processor its relation with the processor with which it interacts
is independent of the syntax and internal structure of that
processor.

It would be useful to have a macro processor which was
embedded in some compiler, or better still in a compiler compiler, which could make use of the syntax analyser and code

generator of that compiler.

To clarify ideas we will give one or two examples and will then consider in more detail some of the implementation problems.

Suppose we have an Algol 60 compiler and would like to build into it some of the features of Algol W (Wirth and Hoare, 1966). For example we may wish to introduce the *while* statement which has syntax

while <logical-expression> *do* <statement>

where as usual "<statement>" can be a simple assignment statement or a complicated block structure provided that it satisfies the definition of a statement in the Algol W language definition. The meaning of this addition to the language is that so long as the <logical-expression> has value "true" the statement part will be repeatedly executed and will be eventually skipped over when the logical expression has value "false". If the logical expression has value "false" on the first entry to the *while* statement then the expression part is not executed at all.

The word *while* is already a reserved word of Algol 60 but is used in a different context. If however this causes the reader any aesthetic difficulty he is advised to change every occurrence of *while* in the rest of this chapter to *whilst*. This will still leave some semantic problems since *whilst* is not a reserved word of Algol W but you cannot have everything!

The *while* statement itself could clearly be regarded as a macro template

while $1 *do* $2

where $1 is assumed to be a logical expression and $2 is a statement and a corresponding macro body written in Algol 60 could be

> label: *if* $1 *then begin* $2*;go to* label *end*

Such a replacement of code could be carried out in a precompilation scan by any general purpose macro processor but there are two distinct disadvantages of this approach. If $1 and $2 are simply copied into the output code then it is up to the user to ensure that they are syntactically correct. The compiler will of course subsequently check the syntax and will produce error messages at this stage if the user is in error and in this simple example it would not be too difficult for the user to associate the error messages from the compiler with his original code but even this assumes some sophistication on the part of the user. It would certainly make the teaching of the *while* statement in an elementary programming course more difficult if this internal replacement had to be explained and would take away much of the advantage of the "cleaness" of the *while* statement as a programming tool. Debugging would however be even more difficult if the *while* statement was now embedded in some other macro body of which the unsophisticated user had no knowledge and clearly the greater depth to which the embedding takes place, the more and more obscure the error messages become. It would not even be possible to completely debug the inner macros since their own parameters may well be dependent on the user supplied parameters of the outermost call.

The second and equally important deficiency of this simple minded approach is that the eventual compilation of the output code from the preprocessor could be very inefficient. In the example just given this is not so, but if the macro body had, for example, contained several instances of the parameter $2 then this statement would be independently syntax checked and corresponding code generated on each of its appearances in the macro body since the compiler would have no information about its origin.

As a second example we will consider the Algol W *case of* structure.

This can take one of two basic forms. First we can have

case <integer-expression> *of begin* <statement-list> *end*

which is of the case-statement type. The execution of this statement proceeds in the following steps:

1. Evaluate the integer-expression of the case clause.
2. Execute the statement in the statement-list whose ordinal number is equal to the value obtained in step 1. If there are n separate statements in the statement-list and the value obtained in step 1 is not in the range 1 to n inclusive then the case statement is not defined and a run time error is deemed to have occurred.

A simple example of a case-statement is

```
case I of
        begin X:=X+Y;
                Y:=X+Y;
                begin A:=B;
                        C:=D
                end
        end
```

where if I has value 1 at execution time then the statement X:=X+Y; is obeyed whereas if I has value 3 then the block (statement)

```
        begin A:=B;
                C:=D
        end
```

is obeyed and if I does not have one of the values 1, 2 or 3 then a run time error occurs.

The second type of case structure is the case-expression type which has syntax

case <integer-expression> of (<T-expression-list>)

where T can be any of the words

integer	logical
real	bit
long-real	string
complex	reference
long-complex	

The execution of a case-T-expression is similar to that of the case-statement and proceeds in the following steps.

1. Evaluate the integer-expression of the case clause.
2. Select and evaluate the T-expression whose ordinal number in the T-expression list is equal to the value obtained in step 1. If there are n separate T-expressions in the T-expression-list and the value obtained in step 1 is outside the range 1 to n inclusive then a run time error is deemed to have occurred. The expressions in the T-expression-list are separated by commas.

Two obvious examples which need no further explanation are write
(case I of ("SPADES ", "HEARTS ", "DIAMONDS", "CLUBS   "));
or
    VAT := PRICE * case VATRATE of (8.0, 10.0, 25.0)/100.0;

The same problems as in the "while" example above apply to

both the *case* structures with the added complication that the macro body becomes much more difficult to write. It should be remembered that the selection of the appropriate statement or T-expression does not take place until run time and therefore cannot be handled at macro expansion time. More efficient code could probably be produced by writing the macro bodies in some lower level language than Algol 60 but this would require a knowledge of the inner workings of the Algol 60 compiler particularly for the case-expression structure. In addition the run time diagnostics and job termination would require careful handling.

One further example to illustrate the difficulty of extending Algol 60 to Algol W is in the data structure area. In Algol W it is possible to declare and manipulate string variables. We can for example declare a string of length 100 with name S by the declaration

   string (100)S;

and similarly an array of strings of length 10 can be declared by

   string (10) *array* TOWN (1::100)

giving a possibility of maintaining a list of up to 100 towns with names consisting of not more than 10 characters each. It must also be possible to manipulate strings and a variety of string operators are available. Just one example will suffice here. It is possible to pick out a substring from a string by using the rule

   <substring-designator> ::= <string variable>
                  (<integer-expression><bar><integer-constant>)

183

where <bar> is a vertical bar (note that we have an ambiguity problem with the BNF metasyntactic language here) and where the evaluated integer-expression gives one less than the ordinal number of the first character in the required substring and the integer-constant denotes the substring length. There are again error conditions but we will not consider them here.

Now for example we can write

S(49|2)

to pick out the substring consisting of the 50th and 51st character from S and similarly

TOWN(20)(0|3)

would pick out the first three characters in the 20th town.

Clearly the problems of implementing an extension of this type are much more complex and fundamental than those in the previous two examples.

We will discuss in the remaining sections of this chapter some proposals which have been made to allow the use of various parts of a compiler in an associated macro processor.

7.2   *Basic concepts and definitions*

There are three different levels at which a macro processor can be integrated into a compiler. Firstly, as we have seen in earlier chapters, there is the preprocessor or lexical analysis phase. A preprocessing macro processor is essentially independent of any particular compiler whereas a lexical analysis phase macro processor must be integrated at this level. This is not very difficult but makes it system dependent rather than general purpose. Clearly it requires a knowledge of and modification to the lexical analyser. Most assembler language macro processors come into this category.

The second possible point of integration is at the syntactic analysis phase. Here the existing syntactic and corresponding semantic structure may be used and this in itself greatly extends the power of the macro processor, at least as a special purpose processor in the application area of the base language. In addition however, it may be possible to extend the base language by the introduction of new syntactic structures together with corresponding semantics.

Finally integration may be achieved at the code production phase where, for example, open coding may be introduced for various procedures and functions and some degree of optimisation may be achieved.

These three phases are not necessarily independent and some degree of overlap will usually exist. Clearly a macro processor integrated at the second or third phase involves an intimate knowledge of the associated compiler and also a compiler design which permits this integration. We will suppose a compiler model with the following basic components:

    lexical analyser
    syntactic analyser
    parse interpreter
    optimiser
    code generator
    formatter and output generator.

These parts will not usually be independent of one another but should be capable of identification in a well structured compiler.

There are also usually three distinct languages associated with a compiler. The first of these is the basic language Lb in which the user programs are written and whose syntax is being checked by the syntactic analysis phase of the compiler. The syntax of a preprocessor or lexical analysis phase macro pro-

cessor only needs to be compatible with Lb at the macro call
level. This can be very trivial in the case in which some
reserved character is used to signal the initiation of a macro
call.

A macro processor introduced at the syntactic analysis
phase needs minimally to be able to communicate with the syntax
analyser but for efficiency and flexibility will also need
knowledge of the descriptive language Ld which is used to describe the syntax and semantics of Lp and to interpret the
parse. Thus Ld could be the metalanguage of BNF together with
facilities for representing the effect of different syntactic
constructs. These facilities may be described in the language
or else some other target language of the compiler. It is
possible for Lb to be the target machine code language but
more generally it is some system language with an overlying
Algol-like structure but with more basic capabilities such as
stack or register manipulation included. The use of macro
generators at the code generation phase involves the final
translation to the target language.

If the language Lb is to be extended by the use of syntax macros or by some other means we will obtain a new language
which will usually contain Lb. We will regard this as
the current programming language for the user and will refer
to it as Lp. Note that before extension takes place Lp is
identical with Lb and as extensions are made, Lp itself expands with each new language Lp containing the previous one
as a subset. If the meaning of each extension is written in
the existing Lp then it follows that after macro expansion the
code generated is expressed solely in Lb.

7.3   *Syntax macros at the syntactic analysis phase*
We will suppose in this section that any language extensions do not involve a modification of the grammar of the
language Lb. The *while* statement of Algol W described above

comes into this category in relation to Algol 60 since the corresponding macro body can be written entirely in Algol 60. Even if the macro body after substitution of the call time parameters is to be returned to the compiler for rescanning, we have already progressed from the macro generators described in earlier chapters since the syntactic types of the actual parameters need to be checked before substitution. The first thing therefore that a syntax macro generator must do on recognising a macro call is to check the types of the actual parameters. Assuming that these are correct it would then simply substitute them into the macro body which would be returned for rescanning. This would be very inefficient since even in the simple case of the *while* statement a parameter would be analysed twice, once to verify its type before substitution and once during the scanning of the macro body after parameter substitution.

To illustrate this inefficiency problem more convincingly we will give another example. Suppose we have defined a macro template to sum a number of terms as follows

sum in <variable> of <expression> with
        <variable> from <expression> to <expression>

A typical call might be

sum in T of A[k] with k from 1 by 1 to 10.

We can make use of the *while* macro as an inner macro call in the following macro body.

```
begin $1 := 0; $3 := $4;
    while $3 ≤ $6 do
        begin $1 := $1 + $2;
            $3 := $3 + $5
        end
    end                                             187
```

On making the macro call

sum in T of A[k] with k from 1 by 1 to 10

it can be seen that a great deal of unnecessary syntax checking
will occur. The inner macro call will become

while k ≤ 10 *do*
    begin T := T + A[k];
        k := k + 1
  end

and each of k, 10 and the statement block will be scanned again
to verify that they are of the right syntactic type for the
while macro. In particular the variable k will be scanned six
times to verify that it is an integer variable. The situation
becomes even worse if we utilise macros to greater depths as is
very common in any well used macro environment.

Furthermore, a very natural thing to do might be to form
the row sums A[j] and the total sum T of the elements of B[j,k]
by writing

Sum in T of
(Sum in A[j] of B[j,k] with k from 1 by 1 to 20)
with j from 1 by 1 to 10.

The amount of redundant work to be done in syntax checking
is enormous, but the result would be that the outer macro would
reject its second parameter because it is not of type <expres-
sion>. Even if the inner sum macro were expanded first it would
still not be of type <expression> and so the outer macro expansion attempt would fail. This indicates how careful one must be
in making a facility of this type generally available.

It should be pointed out here however that one problem,

namely that of inexplicable error messages relative to the outer macro call appearing for the unsophisticated user, is already solved since if the parameters do not syntax check then an error message relative to the macro call itself can be given.

Yet more problems however arise with an attempt to implement the *case* structures defined in section 7.1. Any attempt to implement these directly using Algol 60 as a base language would necessarily be clumsy although possible. Another problem may occur with the error condition which can arise at run time and although again this can be handled within the Algol 60 language the solution is not very satisfactory.

The situation is even worse if we try to implement string declaratives and operators.

7.4   *Code macros*

One method of overcoming the problems of inefficiency outlined above is to produce partially compiled code as the type of each parameter is being verified and also to partially compile, once and for all, the macro body itself but still leaving "holes" for the actual parameters. This is fairly straightforward if conditional macro time statements are not used in the macro body and we will give an example shortly. There is however another problem which we must consider immediately. As we have noted above, if we generate code on recognition of a macro call during the original parse, then that parse will have no indication of the syntactic type of the code generated and it cannot continue sensibly without this information. Thus in the *while* example, the analyser must be informed that the *while...do* macro corresponds to a <statement> syntactic type and it must be able to use this information as if it had found it out for itself. This information can often be declared at macro definition time so instead of the conventional template declaration

```
MACRO while <logical-expression> do <statement>
```

we could write

```
SMACRO while <logical-expression> do <statement>
AS <statement>
label : if $1 then
          begin $2;
              go to label
        end
```

where the word SMACRO informs the macro processor that a syntax macro is about to be defined and the line

```
AS <statement>
```

informs the syntax analyser that the macro body is of syntactic type <statement> so far as the language Lp is concerned.
This raises another problem as to whether or not this declared
type of the macro body is to be checked against the body itself. In simple cases this can be done at macro declaration
time but in more complex situations involving conditional assembly at macro expansion time it may not be possible to do
this until expansion time when the actual parameters are known.
The simplest solution is to put the onus on the writer of the
macro body to ensure that its declared type is correct but this
could be dangerous in general use. For this reason it is usual
to restrict language extension of this type to the professional
programmer and to make his extensions and not the extension
mechanism itself available to the general user.

There is no reason why the type of the macro body should
be restricted to <statement> as in the while macro. More generally the form of an SMACRO will be

```
SMACRO <macro template>
AS <syntactic type>
<macro body>
```

To return to the example of the *while* statement, in order
to write a macro body in semi-compiled code we need first to
define such a code. We will use here the β-machine of Randell
and Russell (Randell and Russell, 1964) but those who are not
familiar with this notation should not find it too difficult
to understand the idea with the help of the following brief
sketch of the β-machine.

The β-machine is a stack machine and whenever a command
TIR <variable name> is used in a β-machine program it simply
means that the corresponding integer value or "result" is to
be placed on the stack. Similarly an operator such as + or
< means that the operator is to be applied to values on top
of the stack and its result is to replace those values on the
stack.

Thus a β-machine program

1.   TIR A
2.   TIR B
3.   +
4.   TIR C
5.   *
6.   TIR D
7.   >

is equivalent to the evaluation of the logical expression

(A+B) * C > D

and its effect is to leave the value true or false on the
stack. Similar arithmetic with reals will be carried out if

the operator TRR is used.

To illustrate our example we need two other instructions which control branches and two to assign values to variables. These are

UJ (n)

which is an unconditional branch to the instruction in line number n and

IFJ (n)

which is a conditional jump to line number n, the condition being that if the value on top of the stack is false then the jump takes place and if it is true then processing continues sequentially. In both cases, the boolean value on top of the stack is deleted. Thus in the example above if a line 8 defined by

8. IFJ (20)

is introduced then the jump to line 20 occurs if and only if

$$(A+B) * C \leq D$$

For assignment of values we need firstly an operator to put an address on the stack. This is

TRA X

to put the address of the real variable X on the stack with a similar one, namely

TIA J

to handle the address of an integer variable J.

On completion of the calculation of the right hand side of an assignment statement we expect to find an address and a value in the top two positions on the stack. The β-machine operator

ST

will now store this value in the corresponding address and will delete these two items from the stack. Thus

TRA A
TRR B
ST

corresponds to the assignment statement

A := B;

If we now consider the SMACRO

SMACRO *while* <logical-expression> *do* <statement>
AS <statement>
label : *if* $1 *then* *begin* $2;*go* *to* label *end*

then the macro body could be semi-compiled at macro definition time to

1. $1 (to be filled in later)
2.   IFJ (5)
3. $2 (to be filled in later)
4.   UJ (1)
5.   . . . .

When the actual parameters $1 and $2 are given at run time the
gaps can be filled in but clearly there is a difficulty here
since $1 and $2 are unlikely to compile into single instructions and so the labelling of instructions will go wrong. The
simplest way to overcome this is to modify the β-machine to
issue unique labels and also, to avoid too much passing of information between macros, to permit simple expressions such as
L1 + 1 with obvious meaning. Thus the macro body above would
now semi-compile to

```
L1 : $1
       IFJ (L2 + 1)
       $2
L2 : UJ (L1)
```

Note also that during semi-compilation of the macro
body it is possible to verify that provided $1 is of type
<logical-expression> and $2 is of type <statement> then the
corresponding macro body will be of type <statement>.

At run time the macro call

```
while (I<J) ∧ (I≠K) do
        begin A:=A+B;
               I:=I+J
        end
```

will result in parameters $1 and $2 semi-compiling to

```
    TIR I
    TIR J
     <
    TIR I
    TIR K
     ≠
     ∧
```

and

```
            TRA A
            TRR A
            TRR B
             +
            ST
            TIA I
            TIR I
            TIR J
             +
            ST
```

respectively. The complete β-machine code output would now be

```
    L1 :    TIR I
            TIR J
             <
            TIR I
            TIR K
             ≠
             ∧
            IFJ (L2+1)
            TRA A
            TRR A
            TRR B
             +
            ST
            TIA I
            TIR I
            TIR J
             +
            ST
    L2      UJ (L1)
```

The statement part would have been more sensible if we had used subscripted variables but we have avoided this so as to keep our β-machine description simple. It is easy to extend the language to cover this possibility.

There are still some problems to be solved if this method is to be used. Firstly there is the problem of inner macro calls. It is fairly simple to modify the β-machine to handle the internal mechanism of a call to another macro at macro expansion time but some method of parameter passing has to be devised. The parameters of an inner macro call will usually be constructed from some or all of the parameters of the outer call and if these are already in semi-compiled code then they cannot be immediately recognised to be of the right syntactic type by the inner macro. It is undesirable to fully expand all inner macro calls at macro definition time since this unnecessarily restricts the flexibility of the system and it would be very inefficient as indicated above to pass the original parameter code for rescanning. One simple method would be to pass some internal marker which would have the dual property of indicating the parameter syntactic type to the inner macro and simultaneously acting as a pointer to the semi-compiled actual parameter for subsequent substitution in the inner macro body. This would require careful construction of both the syntactic analysis phase of the compiler and of the macro system itself but could lead to a very efficient system since actual substitution of code for the parameters need not take place until return to the outermost macro call.

Another problem concerns the generality of the extension mechanism available if the above method is used. We have implied earlier that the macro bodies will usually be written in the programming language Lp but this restricts the extensions to operations which can be programmed in Lp. It not only restricts the scope of such operations but can also make them very inefficient. For example it would be possible to introduce bit handling operations into Fortran IV but the resulting code could not be other than inefficient.

We can overcome both of these last two points by allowing code macro bodies to be written as we please so that in our example above, the code would be the β-machine language rather than Algol 60. We will not develop this idea further but will leave it as part of a possible group project for developing a syntax macro generator.

In this section we have introduced the idea of writing code bodies of macros in a language other than Lp. In our case we have chosen the β-machine language of Randell and Russell since this is quite easy to understand and was useful for illustrating the ideas. Most compilers utilise some internal language which is eventually translated into machine code and clearly any such language can be used for writing code bodies. There are also many different ways of describing semantics, none of which is completely satisfactory. The problem of introducing completely new data types and associated operations which cannot be described in terms of the existing data types in Lp is a difficult problem and one which has not been completely solved. As a research topic it is beyond the scope of this book.

7.5 *Summary*

Syntax macros introduce a new and more flexible property of macro parameters. By delaying their expansion until the syntax analysis phase of compilation it is possible to utilise the syntax checker to verify that the actual parameters are of the syntactic type declared in the template at macro definition time. This means that expressions or assignment statements can for example be given as actual parameters of macro calls. The main problem arising from implementing this idea is that the inefficiency of the system is likely to get worse as the nested depth of macros increases since unless

special precautions are taken, the same piece of code may be
scanned several times in the course of syntax checking. This
can be overcome by passing internal markers which indicate the
syntactic type and location of the corresponding semi-compiled
code. This means that the compiler must be modified to handle
non-terminals as well as terminals in its input string.

It is also useful if a syntactic type can be associated
with a macro body so that repeated scanning of that body can
be avoided. To make this technique of real value it is also
necessary to be able to semi-compile the macro body leaving
only "holes" for the actual parameters to be fitted into. The
system also becomes more powerful if a choice is given to the
writer of macros to use either the programming language Lp or
the internal intermediate language of the compiler for writing
his macro bodies. This degree of flexibility makes it very
easy for mistakes to be made and it is probably best with such
a powerful system to only make its full power available to
professional programmers. It would be quite possible however
to allow macros to be written by the less sophisticated user
provided that the syntactic type of the macro body can be
checked at macro declaration time, assuming of course that the
parameters are of the declared syntactic type.

Language extensions fall into two broad classes, namely
grammatical extensions and data type extensions. As an example of the first of these, the while statement of Algol W
can be added to Algol 60 using only the syntax already available in that language and the *case of* grammatical structures
can be added either within the framework of Algol 60 or else
by using the internal language of the compiler. In both cases
the extension is essentially syntactic.

On the other hand, the introduction of *strings* or *record*
classes are both data type extensions and these are essentially
semantic extensions, and are consequently much more difficult
to handle automatically.

7.6 *Bibliography*

Most of the ideas in this chapter originated in two
papers published independently in 1966. The first of these
by T.E. Cheatham includes a lot of descriptive material about
compilers and macro processors which is now very familiar to
computer scientists but he also introduces the idea of the
smacro which includes the declaration of the syntactic type
of the macro body. The second paper by B.M. Leavenworth is
much shorter and more concise but consequently contains less
technical detail. Leavenworth also introduces smacros but in
his case they mean "statement macros" which imply that the
macro body is of type <statement>. He also introduces fmacros
which are of type <function> but does not press the idea any
further. Both of these papers are worth reading as supplement-
ary material to this chapter.

Backus, J.W. *et. al.* Revised report on the algorithmic language Algol 60; pp. 420-53. *Num. Math.* 4, 1963.

Cheatham, T.E. The introduction of definitional facilities
into higher level programming languages; pp. 623-37.
Proc. AFIPS, 1966; *Fall Joint Computer Conference,* 29,
1966.

Leavenworth, B.M. Syntax macros and extended translation;
pp. 790-3. *Comm. ACM,* 9 (11), 1966.

Randell, B. and Russell, D.J. *Algol 60 Implementation.*
Academic Press, London, 1964.

Wirth, N. and Hoare, C.A.R. A contribution to the development of Algol. *Comm. ACM,* 9 (6), 1966.

7.7 *Examples*

It is difficult to set simple examples on this material
other than examination type questions such as

"Discuss the concept of syntax macros as outlined by ..."

A very interesting group programming project can however
be based on the design of a simple compiler with syntax macro

facilities. It would be instructive to discuss carefully the
type of compiler to be implemented and the "hooks" which are
required to build in a syntax macro processor. The syntax
macro processor should be written by a separate group to the
compiler group to ensure that the interface is clearly defined. The language to be compiled is not very important
although it might be interesting to make it a simple interactive arithmetic language which could then be extended using
the macro processor.

8 · Some applications of syntax macros to extensible compilers

8.1   *Introduction*

In the previous chapter we have discussed the ideas introduced independently by Cheatham and Leavenworth for syntax macro processors. We saw there that it was necessary to integrate the macro processor with the compiler, preferably at both the syntactic analysis and code production phases. An actual implementation requires either a very well constructed existing compiler or else a new one specially written with the introduction of syntax macros in mind. In this chapter we discuss three implementations of syntax macros leading to extensible compilers.

The first of these relates to the compiler for the programming language BALM which is an ALGOL-like language with the object of simplifying list processing operations and making them available to a wider programming population than hitherto. The compiler was specially written for this purpose and with the possibility of extensions using syntax macros in mind.

The second is a syntax macro system which has been built on top of the Manchester revised compiler compiler. In a sense, this compiler compiler is already a vehicle for extensible languages since one may update and recompile previously defined languages at will but the ideas discussed in this chapter make an extension mechanism available to a very wide class of user from the relatively inexperienced to the professional programmer.

Finally we describe an extension mechanism built on top

of another existing compiler, this time for a language specifically designed for the systems programmer. This language
was designed and implemented at the Grenoble IBM Scientific
Centre, now unhappily defunct, and is known as GSL (Grenoble
Systems Language).

Our main interest, as in the rest of this book will be
in the implementation techniques and in an assessment of how
far the objectives described in the previous chapter have been
achieved in these implementations.

8.2   *BALM - an extendible list processing language*

The language BALM (*B*lock *A*nd *L*ist *M*anipulator) has been
defined and implemented by M.C. Harrison (1970). Its main interest to us is in the extension mechanism but in order to
understand this it is necessary to give a brief description of
some of the features of the base language. Fuller details are
given in Harrison's paper.

The BALM language itself is an Algol-like language with
data objects of various types including list, vector and string
and with simple read and print commands. It was designed to
"bring list processing to the masses, as well as to create a
seductive and extendible language". Internally it is converted
to a LISP like language (McCarthy, 1962) which is subsequently
interpreted in a manner similar to the interpretation of LISP
1.5.

A BALM program consists of a sequence of commands separated by semi-colons such as

A=1.2;

or

PRINT(A);

with obvious meaning. Values of expressions may be assigned
to variables using the usual arithmetic operators. Thus

    X = A * B + 4.0/C;

is permissible if A,B,C have been assigned some real values.
Data types are not formally declared and automatic type conversion is carried out where necessary.

A list is always enclosed in round brackets and the elements of the list are separated by spaces excepting that if the
element is itself a list then, being enclosed in brackets, no
extra delimiting space is required.

Thus

    (A(B C)D E)

is a list with elements

    A   (B C)   D   E

The assignment of a list (or, as we shall shortly see, a
vector) to a variable is preceded by an inverted double quote
character as follows

    X = "(A(B C)D E);

with meaning in a more conventional notation

    X = LIST(A,LIST(B,C),D,E);

The prefix operators HD and TL, having the same effect as
the LISP operators CAR and CDR can be applied to lists so that

    PRINT(HD HD TL X);

would print

B

The LISP CONS operator is available as an infix colon associating to the right. The list assigned to X above could also have been assigned in a more clumsy way as follows

X = "A "(B C) : "D:"E:NIL;

or

X = A:LIST(B,C):D:E:NIL;

Vectors may be assigned in a similar way to lists but using square brackets instead of round brackets as delimiters and vectors of vectors, vectors of lists, lists of vectors and various mixtures are permitted. Character strings enclosed in angled brackets may also be defined and manipulated.

In the BALM system properties may be assigned to variables. The command

"VAR PROP "ABCD = <STR>;

assigns the property with name ABCD and associated value <STR> to the variable VAR and subsequently

X = "VAR PROP "ABCD;

will set the value of X to the value of the property ABCD of variable VAR.

BALM also contains a procedure defining and using mechanism which is particularly interesting since it is regarded as another type of data object which can be assigned as the value of a variable. For example

SUMSQ = PROC (X,Y), X↑2 + Y↑2 END;

is translated into an internal form to carry out the operation
of summing two squares and the internal code for this is assigned
to the variable with name SUMSQ. Any statement including for
example SUMSQ(2,3) would eventually interpret this as 13.

This very brief description of BALM leaves out many of the
interesting features of the language and a more careful study of
Harrison's paper is recommended to the reader who has a general
interest in languages. However, our interest here is in the
extension mechanism and we can now look at this.

The translation procedure used by BALM is very simple
being in two passes.

The first is a precedence analysis pass with the only
built in syntax being to handle such things as parenthesised
subexpressions, procedure calls and indexing of vectors.

All other syntax information is given in three lists
whose names are UNARYLIST, INFIXLIST and MACROLIST each of
which have a basic set of elements with given priorities but
which can be modified by the user by adding, deleting or change-
ing operators or macros.

Each operator has a precedence value and a semantic procedure or macro associated with it. The basic UNARYLIST contains unary operators such as -, HD and TL together with "bracket" operators such as BEGIN which is terminated by the corresponding infix operator END.

Similarly the basic INFIXLIST contains operators such as
+, * and =.

New operators can be added to the lists UNARYLIST and
INFIXLIST by the system procedures UNARY, BRACKET or INFIX.
Thus

UNARY("ARG1, ARG2, ARG3);

establishes a unary operator with name ARG1, precedence value
ARG2 which must therefore be, or evaluate to, some value with
associated semantics ARG3. Hence

        UNARY("PR, 150, "PRINT);

defines a unary operator with name PR and precedence value
150 and associates it with the already defined system function
PRINT. Note that PR does not replace PRINT but merely gives it
an alternative name with possibly a different precedence value.

Upon completion of the precedence analysis phase the
corresponding syntax tree is analysed into an internal form
which as we have mentioned above is a LISP-like language. We
are not concerned with this internal language here, but readers
who are familiar with LISP will find Harrison's description of
some examples very interesting and easy to read.

The method of analysis of the syntax tree is very simple.
If the root of the tree is a macro then this macro is expanded
by the system function EXPAND using the whole tree as argument.
If the root of the tree is an operator then it can usually be
applied immediately without further expansion. In this case,
the function EXPAND is applied to each of the subtrees of the
root recursively.

There is no reason why a macro should not itself be a
translator for some other language embedded in BALM. Thus a
macro SNOBOL with appropriately defined body could legitimately
call a SNOBOL interpreter within BALM.

One interesting outcome of the method of expansion using
a syntax tree is that the left hand side of an assignment statement need not be just a simple variable. It could for example
be a piece of program which at run time selects a particular
element of an array as the assignment variable.

New macros may be defined also by the "MEANS" operator.
This has syntax

<expr1>MEANS<expr2>

where <expr1> has the precedence of all its operators defined
and <expr2> is a valid expression in BALM. In the notation we
have already defined <expr1> is the template and <expr2> is
the body of the macro we are defining. Formal parameters in
<expr1> are indicated by the variables X1, X2, ..., X10 and the
same symbols are used as parameter markers in <expr2>. At
macro expansion time the actual parameters corresponding to
X1, X2, ..., X10 may be arbitrary expressions.

Thus, for example we could define a macro

FOR X1=X2 TO X3 BY X4 DO X5

MEANS

FOR X1=(X2,X3,X4)REPEAT X5

with obvious meaning. It should be noted that the precedence
of the operators TO, BY and DO must have been previously defined.

We conclude this section with another example to illustrate the use of conditional assembly whereby a single operator
$\oplus$ can be used to imply integer addition or concatenation of
strings, vectors or ordered pairs of items. We will give
three different solutions to this problem to indicate alternative methods of handling the semantics of the extension.

To simplify the programs we will assume that the meaning
to be assigned to the operator $\oplus$ may be determined by looking
at the leftmost operand only. A slightly more complicated
construction would be needed to check both operands. We will
also indicate failure to recognise an operand of appropriate
type by the return of NIL.

Firstly we define the precedence for the new binary operator ⊕ on the left and on the right by a statement

INFIX("⊕, 1501, 1500, "⊕)

This means that the operator ⊕ has left and right precedence of 1501 and 1500 respectively and the second occurrence of ⊕ implies that the semantics do not already exist but will be defined along with the macro for ⊕. This can now be done as follows by the macro definition

```
X1 ⊕ X2 MEANS
    IF STRQ(X1) or VECTQ(X1)
        THEN CONCAT (X1,X2)
    ELSEIF PAIRQ(X1)
        THEN X1 : X2
    ELSEIF INTQ(X1)
        THEN X1 + X2
    ELSE NIL END;
```

The functions STRQ, VECTQ, PAIRQ and INTQ return the value TRUE or FALSE depending on the type of the operand.

Thus after definition of this macro the input

```
PRINT(3⊕4)
PRINT(#HOUND#⊕#DOG#);
PRINT(VECTOR(1,2,3)⊕VECTOR(4,5,6));
PRINT(LIST(1,2)⊕LIST(3,4));
STOP;
```

would produce output

```
7
"HOUNDDOG"
[1,2,3,4,5,6]
((1 2)3 4)
```

The solution to the above is a pure macro expansion solution but it is interesting to see how a similar effect but using a different method can be achieved. This is by the use of procedures which we have not defined but have obvious properties.

With the same infix definition we will firstly define a procedure called PLUS as follows

```
PLUS = PROC (X1,X2),
IF STRQ(X1) OR VECTQ(X1) THEN CONCAT (X1,X2)
ELSEIF PAIRQ(X1) THEN X1 : X2
ELSEIF INTQ(X1) THEN X1+X2
ELSE NIL END;
```

We can now define a macro

```
X1⊕X2 MEANS
PLUS(X1,X2);
```

which simply replaces X1⊕X2 by the procedure call PLUS(X1,X2). The advantage of using this method over that of using a straight procedure call is that the user can write his expressions using the infix notation X1⊕X2.

The final solution is equivalent to the last one but is simpler to define. We only need to define the infix operator ⊕ by

```
INFIX("⊕,1501,1500,"PLUS)
```

which together with the procedure declaration above automatically assigns this meaning to ⊕.

This very brief description does not do full justice to BALM. The main extensibility features apart from the fairly standard definition of procedures are the ability to define new

unary and infix operators with associated semantics, to define
macros and to change the translator either for special purpose
translation within the usual translation process or by changing
the translator itself for the duration of the whole job.

Of these extensions, the ability to introduce new infix
operators with associated semantics is perhaps the most unusual

8.3 *A user extensible language built on to a compiler compile*

The original compiler compiler of Brooker et al (1963)
made extensible language available to the users in the sense th
they could define their language syntactically and semantically
and obtain a compiler for that language by processing it throug
the compiler compiler system. More recently Napper (1967),
using the revised version of the compiler compiler has made
proposals for a language which consists of a simple basic sourc
language which contains a definition mechanism which allows thi
language to be extended indefinitely. The original name proposed by Napper for this language was SNAP (*System for Natural
Programming*) but since SNAP was already in existence as the
name of another programming language, a more recent publication
giving a user's view of an implementation by Napper and Fisher
(1975) has renamed it ALEC (*A Language with an Extensible Com-*
piler).

Extensibility is achieved by using the notation of "forma
and "informal" macros but the really interesting thing about th
process is that extension is implemented by the macro definitio
causing an extension to the compiler itself thus causing macro
calls to be processed in the same way as the base language itself. This requires no macro processing pre-compilation scan
and is thus potentially very efficient.

The base language chosen was a subset of PL/1. Algol 68
was rejected because of the difficulty in breaking down a sourc
program into a set of short statements or clauses due to its l
of distinction between assignment statements and expressions.

210

No reason is given for the rejection of Algol 60 or Algol W as a base language.

Macro definitions must all be made before the actual program which uses them commences. To make this division quite clear the delimiter *BEGIN PROGRAM* must occur between macro definition and the actual program using them. At this point the compiler has already been augmented by the macro definitions and unmarked sections of the revised compiler compiler (RCC) can be discarded and subsequent compilation carried out in the remainder of this single pass.

The minimum knowledge that a user needs to introduce language extensions is some programming ability in the base subset of PL/1 with its ALEC dialect together with the syntax of *formal macros* which is the name given to simple macros of this type.

A formal macro definition is syntactically identical to a procedure declaration except that the word *OPEN* appears at the beginning of the heading. Procedures may be either routines or functions. To illustrate the idea we will consider a routine and only note that functions are handled similarly.

Consider for example the macro definition

OPEN ROUTINE ADD (REAL X) TO (REAL VARIABLE Y) AND
(REAL VARIABLE Z);

    Y = Y + X; Z =Z + X;
END;

The syntactic type *REAL* here applied to X implies that the actual parameter may be a real expression whereas *REAL VARIABLE* Y implies that the actual parameter corresponding to Y must be a real variable. In the example as written above the binding of actual to formal parameters is actually compiled so a subsequent macro call

ADD P + Q * R *TO* S *AND* T;

would compile to

BEGIN; DECLARE (X,Y,Z) *REAL;*
X = P + Q * R; Y = S; Z = T;
Y = Y + X; Z = Z + X;
S = Y; T = Z;
END;

Although the substitution

X = P+Q*R;

introduces some optimisation of run time code, the other two substitutions

Y = S; Z = T;

are inefficient. They can be eliminated by the "true substitution" declaration *TR SUBST* which means that the actual parameter is physically substituted for each occurrence of the formal parameter in the macro body.

Thus the macro template in the above example could have been written

OPEN ROUTINE ADD (*REAL* X) *TO* (*REAL VARIABLE TRSUBST* Y)
AND (*REAL VARIABLE TRSUBST* Z);

with the same macro body and then the same call would have yielded

BEGIN; DECLARE (X) *REAL;*
     X = P + Q * R; S = S + X; T = T + X;
END;

which is much more acceptable code. It should be noted that in ALEC block entry and exit instructions are only compiled if necessary.

The language extension using formal macros is clearly limited to the closed procedure call with semantics written in the existing instructions of ALEC. However, a second class of macros, namely "informal macros" allows for greater freedom in syntactic and semantic extensibility. This is done by allowing the user to write the bodies of his informal macros in RCC rather than just in ALEC. In fact, really only one class of macro actually exists since ALEC automatically converts formal into informal macros.

The detail of how informal macros work is too technical to include here but we will attempt to summarise, without detailed explanation, some of their interesting features.

Firstly an RCC heading allows any symbols as delimiter symbols. Suppose for example that we wished to increment a pointer J by 1 and also to carry out some "housekeeping" functions at the same time. Then a conventional macro processor and indeed the formal macros of ALEC would expect a macro call such as

NEXT J;

where the macro call is delimited by the fixed symbol strings NEXT and ;. However, an informal macro could be defined in ALEC so that whenever an imperative such as J + 1; occurred it would have the effect of incrementing J and initiating the other requirements. In this case the macro template is defined by a statement

[OPEN ALEC PIECE] : [VARIABLE a] + 1;

where [OPEN ALEC PIECE] is a syntactic class which is to be

augmented by the new alternative

$$[\text{VARIABLE } a] + 1$$

with semantics corresponding to the macro body which would
follow the above template.

A second type of extension allows alternative macro templates to be used with the same macro body so that for example

FOR I = I *STEP* 1 *UNTIL* 10 *DO*

and

FOR I *UPTO* 10 *DO*

would both be recognised as the same macro call. This is
equivalent to providing conditional assembly. Variable lists
of parameters can also be handled.

Finally machine code macro bodies can be written by the
user thus releasing him simply from the constraint of writing
his macro bodies in ALEC or RCC. In this way the user with
detailed knowledge of RCC could write macro bodies to make use
of, for example, error handling routines in RCC.

In conclusion we would emphasise again that the most
interesting feature of ALEC is that it uses RCC so that macro
definitions are directly incorporated in the compiler and are
handled just as any other language features. It is this fact
that makes ALEC an efficient extensible system.

8.4   *An extension mechanism for LL(1) languages*

In this section we describe the work of a research student, M. Jorge Vidart of the University of Grenoble which formed part of his Docteur de troisième cycle thesis. Much of
his work was concerned with the general problem of providing
an extension mechanism for any compiler but in particular for

those handling LL(1) grammars and the corresponding languages
as discussed by Lewis and Stearns (1968) and by Rosenkrantz
and Stearns (1969). The main point of interest of LL(1)
grammars in this section is that they can be parsed top-down
and without back-up by examining at each step the next symbol
to the right of the current position. The Grenoble Systems
Language (Berthaud et al, 1972) is a language which provides
the usual tools for systems programming but built into
a PL/1-like framework, with an LL(1) grammar and a top down
compiler utilising this fact.

We will not be concerned with the details of this language but note the following characteristics which are used in
defining the extension mechanism.

Variables of type *pointer* may be declared with their
values being the address of variables of different types previously defined in the program.

A variable may be declared having a memory classification
BASED which means that the memory allocation for this variable
is directly at the command of the programmer.

The operator "→" is used to associate an address with a
"BASED" variable. It is also used in a BNF notation in conjunction with a vertical bar,

$$|\rightarrow$$

to associate semantics with some rule of the grammar. We will
give an example of this use shortly.

In chapter 7 we discussed some of the problems associated
with the implementation of a syntax macro processor. Vidart's
method overcomes two of these problems, namely that of the inefficiency of repeated scanning of parameters both after substitution in the macro body and in inner macro calls and also
that of the determination of the syntactic class to which the

macro body belongs at macro declaration rather than at macro call time.

The base language used for writing the macro bodies is GSL but augmented by all the extensions defined up to the one being currently processed.

The formal mechanism for making extensions to the language can be described in BNF notation by adding an alternative to the syntactic class <sta> which is the root of the "instructions" of the language. The syntactic rules for this are

```
<sta> ::= <ext syntax>
<ext syntax> ::= EXTSYN <ext-rule> ENDEXT
<ext-rule> ::= <class> := <structure>|→ <meaning>
```

In these rules, upper case letters denote terminals and |→ can be read as "with associated meaning".

<structure> is also formally defined but for our purposes it will suffice to say that it corresponds to the macro template, being a concatenation of terminals and non-terminals but with the first element being one or more non-terminals. It follows that infix operators cannot be defined by this mechanism. The <class> type specifies the expected syntactic type of the macro body which is specified by <meaning>. The class type will also be associated with the template specified by <structure>.

Since <meaning> is restricted to being a phrase in the extended language at the moment of definition of this extension then if the grammar has already been augmented by the previous extension then it can itself be syntax checked at this time. It must however be a special type of syntax check which will be carried out since the template contains non-terminal parameters at this moment. The syntax analyser must therefore be constructed to allow this modified analysis. The output from the syntax analyser is normally a syntax tree with leaves being terminal symbols. In our case, some of the leaves will be syntactic types corresponding to the parameters of the template. By carrying out the analysis at this stage one of the possibilities of obscure error messages being given to the confusion of an unsophisticated programmer is avoided. It should be noted however that this can only be done without ambiguity since the macro bodies are written in the partially extended base language and do not involve conditional expansion by means of a special macro language superimposed on the base language.

Another point to be remembered at this syntactic analysis stage is that the original grammar is LL(1) and that if the same compiler is to be used then the extended language must be LL(1) also. Since the analyser is LL(1) and therefore deterministic it is possible to hold a table of possible successor characters for each syntactic class. The analyser only needs to consult this table to see whether or not it can proceed. Thus when the language is being extended it is necessary to check the table entries corresponding to the associated syntactic class to ensure that the first character or possibly group of characters, if these can be associated with each other during the lexical analysis phase, does not already appear in this part of the table. If it does then the attempt to extend the language in this way must be rejected.

Before considering how the semantics implied by the macro body are handled we will discuss the way in which these syntactic extensions are effected.

The fact that a syntactic extension is about to take place is recognised by the analyser with the occurrence of the word EXTSYN. A note is made of the syntactic class of this extension and an attempt is made to modify the grammar itself by the addition of this alternative to the definitions of the existing alternatives for this class. This can be done by subjecting the extended grammar to an analysis similar to the syntax improving device of Foster (1968). The actual procedure used by Vidart uses a similar transformation described by Griffiths and Peltier (1968). The purpose of this transformation is to produce an LL(1) grammar if possible. If not then an error condition is indicated. If the transformation is successful then the "first successor" characters are added to the table mentioned above and the alternatives are added to the grammar itself. In this respect the system is similar to that of the extensible language ALEC described above.

We discuss now the way in which the semantics or meaning of an extension is handled. Being written in the partially extended language and since the base grammar is modified as each extension is added, the macro body can itself be analysed provided that the analyser can handle syntactic types as possible leaves of the syntax tree as described above. If at the same time as the syntactic analyser extensions are being made, the corresponding semantic routines are added to those for the base language, then an abstract program corresponding to the macro body can be produced with pointers to the various semantic procedures that it uses and also places for pointers to the abstract subprograms corresponding to the actual parameters which will be supplied and similarly expanded at macro call time. This abstract program tree structure is then built into the final abstract program by an integration routine which fills in the pointers to the already semi compiled actual parameters which are themselves abstract program tree structures. The final process is for the interpreter routine to traverse the completed abstract program tree executing on its way the various semantic routines indicated by pointers at the nodes.

We conclude this section with some examples illustrating the different parts of the process described above. Suppose first of all that part of the grammar consists of the rule

A := aB|cD

Then the corresponding part of the syntax analyser could be

```
            ROUTINE A
            DECIDE L1, SINGLE, a
            CHECK (c)
            CALL D
            EXIT
     L1     CHECK (a)
            CALL B
            RETURN
```

where, since the grammar is LL(1) the route through this routine is unambiguously decided by the command

```
            DECIDE L1, SINGLE, a
```

Suppose now that we wish to add an alternative to the definition of class A say

```
      A := xY
```

Then this can be done by the mechanism involving

```
      EXTSYN <A>   := x<Y> |-...... ENDEXT
```

where ..... represents the semantics of this extension. The modified syntax analyser would now be

```
            ROUTINE A
            DECIDE L1, SINGLE, x
            DECIDE L2, SINGLE, a
            CHECK (c)
            CALL D
```

```
        EXIT
L1      CHECK (x)
        CALL Y
        EXIT
L2      CHECK (a)
        CALL B
        RETURN
```

Note that this solution implies that the new definition has been put at the head of the alternatives.

It is also interesting to note that semantic routines can be inserted at this point with no extra overhead. For example if a rule

$$E := a[P]F$$

is to be handled where P is the name of some semantic action to be taken but E and F are syntactic class names then a similar process to that giving the subprogram above would also produce

```
        ROUTINE E
        CHECK (a)
        CALL P
        CALL F
        RETURN
```

but where

```
        CALL P
```

now introduces the required semantic action.

8.5 *Conclusions*

In each of the three extensible languages discussed in this section the emphasis has been on syntactic extension with of course associated semantics but none of them includes true semantic extension with the introduction of essentially new data types with their associated operators. This problem is a very difficult one and it is arguable as to whether or not extensibility through macro processors is the right way to tackle this problem.

Although in the future new and more powerful extensible languages will almost certainly be designed it is of some interest to know that a start has been made with the systems described here and with other extensible compilers which no doubt exist already. The detail of the techniques described here have been different although they are all basically examples of the implementation of syntactic macro systems interfaced with compilers.

The BALM compiler is based on precedence analysis and for this reason it is easy to introduce new infix operators with associated semantics. The language is closely associated with list processing but the techniques employed will be applied in other problem areas.

ALEC relies on the revised compiler compiler for its base and caters for both the sophisticated and unsophisticated user with its informal and formal macro mechanism. Its efficiency comes from the application of compiler compiler techniques to obtain a full independent compiler for the extended language.

Jorge Vidart's system is aimed at system programming and is based on the Grenoble Systems Language GSL and again produces a modified compiler/interpreter for each extended language. Semantics are described only in the previously extended GSL but the syntax of Leavenworth's system has been carefully implemented and precautions taken to make this implementation more efficient than that implied by Leavenworth's proposals.

A great deal of work remains to be done in this area, not only in solving the problem of true semantic extensions but also in the definition of a flexible but efficient base language and a unified theory for the description of syntax and semantics.

8.6 *Bibliography*

Most of the work described in this chapter has been taken from research papers. Most of these are available in generally available computing journals but a few are published only in internal reports. A full list is given here for completeness and the reader who is looking for some interesting research and development problems is strongly advised to study as many as possible.

Berthaud, M., Clauzel, D. and Jacolin, M. Grenoble system language, definition du language. IBM centre scientifique de Grenoble, Etude no. FF2.0133, 1972.

Brooker, R.A. *et al*. The compiler compiler. *Ann. R. Automatic Programming*, vol. 3, 1963.

Foster, J.M. A syntax improving program, p. 31. *Comp. J.* vol. 11, no. 1, 1968.

Foster, J.M. *Automatic syntactic analysis*. MacDonald/Elsevier computer monograph, 1970.

Griffiths, M. and Peltier, M. Grammar transformation as an aid to compiler production. IBM centre scientifique de Grenoble, Etude no. FF2.0057.0, 1968.

Harrison, M. BALM - an extendable list processing language, pp. 507-11. *ACM Spring Joint Computer Conference*, 1970.

Harrison, M., Rubin J. and Albert, D. BALM user's manual. Courant Institute, New York University, 1970.

Lewis, P.M. and Stearns, R.E. Syntax directed transductions, pp. 465-88, *JACM*, 15, 1968.

McCarthy, J. *et al*. *LISP 1.5 Programmer's Manual*. MIT Press, 1962.

Napper, R.B.E.   Some proposals for SNAP, a language with formal macro facilities, pp. 231-43. *Comp. J.* vol. 10, no. 3, 1967.

Napper, R.B.E. and Fisher, R.N.   ALEC - a user extensible scientific programming language. *Comp. J.* (in course of publication), 1975.

Rosenkrantz, D.S. and Stearns, R.E.   *Properties of deterministic top down grammars*, pp. 165-80, ACM symposium on theory of computing, 1969.

Vidart, J.   Extensions syntaxiques dans une contexte LL(1). University of Grenoble.   Thèse pour obtenir le grade de Docteur de troisième cycle, 1974.

Index

The items marked with an * appear frequently throughout the book and only the more important references to them are recorded.

Abstract machine 111
Albert, D. 222
ALEC 210-14, 218, 221
  *formal and informal macros 210-11, 213
  Open Alec piece 213
  true substitution declaration 212
*ALGOL 1-2, 110, 160, 189, 197, 201, 211
ALGOL68 210
ALGOLW 161, 179-94, 211
Ampersand, use of in assembly macros 28, 32
APL 49
Arguments (*see* parameters)
*Assemblers
  *attribute reference 36, 41-5
  conditional statements 29, 33-5, 39
  declarative statements 25
  default options 31
  global variables 39
  IBM/360 21-45, 93
  keyword parameters 30-2
  local variables 37
  looping 37
  macro definition 26
  null parameters 32
  one address 9
  operation code part 22
  parameter lists 32-3
  programming benefits of macros 20-1
  sequence symbols 33
  system functions 32-6
  system macros 45
  three address 9
Atoms 85
Automatic register management 41-2

Backus, J.W. (*see also* BNF) 199
Balanced parameters 137, 144, 157
Ball, W.W.R. 72, 107
BALM 202-9
Base register 22, 24
Bashkow, T.R. 124, 131
BASIL 158
BCPL 131
Berthaud, M. 215, 222
BNF 135, 184, 186, 216
Bootstrapping (*see also* half bootstrap) 99-100, 111, 160-77
Brooker, R.A. 210, 222
Brown, P.J. 19, 49, 85, 99, 102, 107, 109
Byte 21, 24

Campbell, W. vi
case of structure 181-2
Catalogued data set 45
Chain structures 150-4
Cheatham, T.E. 199, 201
Clauzel, D. 222
Code body of a procedure 1
Coleman, S.S. 113, 131
*Compiler 163-75, 178, 201-33
Compiler compiler 201, 211-14, 221
Complex arithmetic 12
*Concatenation of strings 31-2

Data base 156
Data type extensions 198
Declarative statements 3, 25
Deutsch, L.P. 49, 107
Dot and cross products 146-50

Elegant solutions 18
Extended instruction set 23
Extensible compilers 201-33

FLUB (*see also* STAGE2 and SIMCMP) 112-32
    control instructions 121
    flag 120
    pointer 120
    registers 122-3
    value 120
Fisher, R.N. 210, 222
Fortran 1, 110, 159, 160-75, 197
Foster, J.M. 218, 222
Freeman, D.N. 46
Friets, J. 124, 131
Frisbology 6-7

Garbage collection 61
GPM 49, 74–85, 105–7
    actual parameters 75
    conditional statements 79
    copy (quote) mode 75–6
    environment chain 76, 79, 82–5
    formal parameters 75
    F, P, E chains 82–5
    internal structures 81–5
    macro name 75
    successor function 79
    system macros 79
    update function 75
    value function 75
Greenwald, I. 4, 19
Gries, D. 19
Griffiths, M. 218, 222
GSL (and GSL extensions) 214–21
    abstract program tree 218
    BASED classification 215
    EXTSYN extension mechanism 228
    syntax tree 216–18

Half bootstrap 111
Hand coding 175
Harrison, M.C. 202, 205, 222
Hash tables 99
Henninger 124
Hexadecimal numbers 43

IBM/360 architecture 21
IBM/360 assembler language (*see* Assemblers, IBM/360)
IBM literature 46
Idling function in TRAC 59

Jacolin, M. 222
Job Control Language 45–6

Kent, W. 41–2, 46
Kerson, A. 124, 131
Keyword parameters 30–2, 88
Keyword parameter default options 31

Label 28–9
Leavenworth, B.M. 199, 201, 221
Lexical analysis 184
Lewis, P.M. 215, 222
*Library macros 27
Linkage 20
Linked list 61

 LISP 162, 176, 202, 206
*Lists of parameters 27, 39, 136, 142
*List processing 160-77, 201-10
 List structure 115
 Literal equivalence 11, 91
 Literal value 103
 LL(1) grammars 215, 217-19
 Logical connectives 34

 Machine code 168, 172
 Mandil, S.H. 133, 155-8
*Macro
   *body 9
   *call 11, 14, 25
   *definition 3, 8, 26
   *expansion 8-11, 19
    free format 14
    general purpose 85
    internal 12
    library 27
   *name 8-9, 13
   *nested 12, 128
    problem oriented 20
   *replacement 19
    restricted scope 13-14
   *template 4, 8-9
McCarthy, J. 162, 176, 202, 222
McIlroy, M.D. 4, 19
ML/I 49, 50, 85-107
    actual parameters 89
    conditional commands 90-1
    formal parameters 89
    keywords 88
    labels 90
    LOWL 99-105
    LOWL A,B,C registers 101
    LOWL character set 100
    M,T,D options 97
    nodal facility 96
    options 89
    page layout characters 85
    punctuation characters 85
    replacement text 86
    segmentation 86
Mooers, C.N. 49, 59, 63, 66, 107-8
MP3 133-59, 178
    balanced parameters 137, 144, 157
    basic notation 134
    chain map 154
    chains 150-4

command chain 151-3
control statements 141-2
environment chain 157
flagged macro calls 145
global squash length 137
macro name 135
modes of operation 134
separators 136
system markers 136

Napper, R.B.E. 210, 222
*Neutral string 50
*Null string 52, 64, 77, 85, 106

Operation codes (IBM Assembler) 21-6
Optimisation of assembler code 36
Orgass, R.J. 113, 118, 131

Page, E.S. 162, 176
*Parameters 8-9
    *actual 8-9, 16, 28-9
     evaluation 106
    *formal 8-9, 15-16, 28
    *keyword 30
    *list 17, 27
PASCAL 131
Peltier, M. 218, 222
Pengelly, R.M. 157-8
PL/1 133, 160-1, 210, 215
Poel, W. van der 71
Poole, P.C. 110, 112-13, 120, 130-1
Portability 160
Pre-processor 178, 180
Precedence analysis 205, 221
*Procedure 1-2, 20
     call 19
     linkage 1
Punctuation characters 85
Pushdown mode 82

Randell, B. 191, 199
RCC (Revised Compiler Compiler) 211, 213-14, 221
*Recursion 12, 18, 72-5
*Recursive 7, 87, 108
Relational operators 34
Repetitions in ML/1 95
Rosenkrantz, D. 215, 223
Rubin, J. 222
Russell, D.J. 191, 199

Saksena, C.P. 72
Sanders, M. vii
Saunders, R.C. 99
Segmentation 105-6
SIMCMP (*see also* STAGE2 and FLUB) 112-32
    definition end of line flag 114
    parameter flag 114
    source end of line flag 113
SNAP 210
SNOBOL 206
Soft machine (S-machine) 111
Source text 27
*Stacks 2, 81, 98-9, 104, 156, 166, 174, 191-3
*Stack pointer 2, 174
STAGE2 (*see also* FLUB and SIMCOMP) 112-32
    conversion type 124-30
    element weight 126
    macro nesting 127
    tree dictionary 126-7
Stamper, R.K. 157-8
STAMPOL 157
Stearns, R.E. 215, 222-3
Strachey, C. 49, 74, 79, 81, 108
*Strings, character 8, 28, 49-109, 119, 134, 140, 183, 198
Strube, G. 21, 47
Structures of chains 150-4
*Substitution 7
*Syntax 19
*Syntax macros 178-200
    base language, Lb 178, 185-6
    β-machine 191-6
    code macros 189-97
    compiler model 185
  *current programming language Lp 186
    definitions 184-5
  *descriptive language Ld 186
    lexical analysis 184
    semi-compiled parameters 196
    SMACRO 189-97
Syntax rules 17
Systems programming 5

Temple of Benares 71-2
Terminology, definition of 8-12
*Text replacement 3, 5-7, 19
Time sharing 133, 177
Top end macro processor 133, 155, 158
Towers of Hanoi 18, 71-4, 85
TRAC 49-74, 105-7, 178
  *active function 52

*active string 51
  effect 52
  end of segment marker 56
  form store 51
  formal parameter markers 64
  functions 65-8
  idling function 59
  implementation lists 61-2
  internal algorithm 52, 59-61
  internal markers 63
  meta character 52, 70
 *neutral function 52
  pointers 54-5
  primitive functions 51-69
  segments 67
Transporting software 110
Tree oriented dictionary 126-7
Trees 119

Urban Management System 156

Variables (*see* parameters)
Variable length expressions 94
Vidart, J. 214-15, 218, 221, 223
V-type attributes 43

Waite, W.M. 110, 112-13, 118, 120, 130-1, 158
Wegner, P. 19, 108
while statement 179-82, 186-8
Wilkes, M.V. 160-76
Wilson, L.B. 162, 176
Wirth, N. 179
WISP 161-75

Zoned decimal constant 43